MY GURU & I
by
Swami Paranthapa

· PUBLISHING ·

African Perspectives Publishing
PO Box 95342, Grant Park 2051,
Johannesburg, South Africa
www.africanperspectives.co.za

© Patrick Neville Booth

All rights reserved.

No part of this publication may be reproduced, stored in a retrieval system or transmitted in any form or by any means, electronic, mechanical, photocopying or otherwise, without the prior permission of the author and his publisher.

ISBN PRINT: 978-0-6397-8746-6
ISBN DIGITAL: 978-0-6397-8747-3

Cover Image: (From left to right)
Paramahamsa Sri Swami Vishwananda
Swami Paranthapa

Editors: Kristelle Bach Sim (Gauri)
Rose Francis
Proofreader: Richard Gibbs
Scribe: Rohini Dasi (Carol Daglish)
Graphic Designer: Azile Maqwati
Typesetting: Phumzile Mondlani

CONTENTS

PREFACE	7
MY GURU & I	11
SAMADHI	15
THE WATCHER	19
MY GREAT-GRANDMOTHER	25
MY GRANDMOTHER	29
MY FATHER	33
MY MOTHER	35
MOVING TO PIETERMARITZBURG	39
THE ROADMAP TO GOD APPEARS	47
DISCOVERING INTUITIVE ABILITIES	49
HEALING MODALITIES	51
MEETING A YOUNG MAURITIAN SAINT	57
CONNECTING WITH THE MAURITIAN SAINT	63
ORGANISING DARSHAN FOR GURUJI	69
GURUJI MANIFESTS GANESHA	73
MATLAPENG	79
BRAHMACHARI INITIATION	87
CHANGING TRAJECTORIES	97
LEARNING TO TRUST THE GURU	102
MY FIRST VISIT TO INDIA	125
TRIALS BY FIRE	149
BECOMING A SWAMI	165

THE RECKONING	177
A VISION OF LORD KRISHNA	185
AT THE FEET OF THE GURU	191
SEVA TO THE GURU	201
JUST LOVE	207

PREFACE

What a time we live in!

In the external world, it appears as if everything is falling apart. Yet for those who have had the chance to see, meet and truly *know* their Satguru, these fortunate devotees have had the opportunity of experiencing a completely different reality to that which is occurring right now.

Paramhamsa Vishwananda speaks again and again on the importance of having the knowledge that will make it possible for everyone to have a personal relationship with God. His very insistence implies that there is something extraordinary to be gained from that knowledge. And so, with this in mind, the Bhagavad Gita, Srimad Bhagavatam, Guru Gita, and all the books written by Guruji are made available to us as essential resources.

The experiences I've had throughout my life have made it abundantly clear that everything we are looking for is sitting right in front of us in the form of our Satguru. The flow of grace is ubiquitous. The answer to every searching question is held within Him; He is the very embodiment of the Bhagavad Gita, Guru Gita, and Srimad Bhagavatam. He reminds us that He is the perfect reflection of the Love that lies within us; He is the Love we've been waiting to re-discover our whole life.

The Satguru's goal is clear; it is to bring each of us to the awareness of the Divine within us. But what does that require from us?

I once asked Him what it would take to attain Him. He answered, 'It's very easy, and very difficult to gain me. You have just to love me.'

Just loving Him sounds so easy to do. Yet for most of us, it is very difficult because of who we have become. By way of our conditioning, we are accustomed to taking what we can for ourselves. We work hard to serve our desires. This prevents us from loving Him because to truly love Him is to give up our aspirations and serve His agenda. He is here to take us Home, but first, we have to give up our enthrallment with the world. He offers the opportunity to focus on Him and serve Him and in so doing, remember the Love that we are. It is only through Love that we can attain Him. No other way is possible. Just Love.

This relationship takes time to build. As we walk the road, it gets bumpy. We fail to see how He could love us in our current condition. We struggle to trust Him and find it difficult to accept the circumstances He places us in. We misunderstand and fear the concept of surrender. Yet we learn that despite the internal war within us, His Love is unconditional. He loves us through the struggles. He looks beyond our doubts and our self-loathing, to reach into that place within us where He resides. In this way, His presence heals and transforms.

Through this journey with my Guru, I recited these words in times of self-doubt: 'I see what I want in Him, and this means He sees something in me. I can hold onto that; that He sees something valuable in me even if I don't see it in myself.'

When I found my life circumstances difficult or complicated, I felt Him inviting me to wonder, 'Am I prioritising my love relationship with my beloved, with God? Is He the most important to me?'

My life revolves around the continuous presence of my Guru. Everything I get, and everything I don't get, proceeds from Him.

By sharing my experiences with Him, I have the chance to say thank you for the knowledge that is continuously streaming from Him, and for the countless transformations that have taken place so far.

I am because He is ... and this book will show you just how that came to be.

Jai Gurudev

MY GURU & I

Conception

This book was conceived in the middle of the night, in a small town in Maharashtra in 2017. My Guru and I had been travelling across Maharashtra for about a week. I was overcome with appreciation for Sri Swami Vishwananda, and how He had irrevocably transformed my life.

We stopped the car at a chai stand. I looked into His eyes; my heart full of emotions impossible to express. The moment was so incredibly intimate and delicate, all I wanted was to be alone with Him. Knowing my thoughts, He asked the other person in the car to buy us pakora from the chai stand. When she left the car, He took my hands in His, looked at me and said, "You must write about everything you have experienced with me and call it 'My Guru and I'." The moment was so loaded with love, I absorbed the instruction and the journey towards writing this book began.

Back to the beginning

As I look back on my life, I see a sequence of unbelievable circumstances, each following the other to create the story of my destiny; I think about the town where I was born, so far removed from where I find myself now. I recall the events that transpired to transform me from the boy I was then to the man I am today. It has become so clear to me how each one of us is born to walk a path carefully designed to bring about transformational change. Every step we take, every encounter we have, and every situation we find ourselves in, forms part of the tapestry of our destiny.

My childhood relationships brought to the surface all the indispensable qualities that would steer me through the events of my adult life. My mother's affection, her heightened self-confidence; my grandmother's eccentricity and uncompromising fearlessness; my great-grandmother who met my every need as if I were a prince. All of these women played their role in building the strength and resilience that would later be required of me as I walked the road towards my Guru.

Rivers, mountains, and trees were the backdrop to all my adventures. I was carefree, not knowing or caring if there was a different or better way to be. My mother, grandmother, and great-grandmother made for interesting entertainment.

Until I was five years old, I had the presence of both my parents. That changed when my mother moved to focus on her career at nineteen. She felt the responsibility to care for me and that meant seeking opportunities away from the small town of Kokstad, South Africa, where I was born. She left in 1982 to further

her career in Pietermaritzburg. I would see her only sporadically over the next four years.

My life consisted of swimming in rivers and playing scorpion racing with my friends. We climbed a nearby mountainside, scratched around in the dirt for scorpions and put them in a bottle when we caught them. Back then, we were so unafraid. Back down the mountainside, crossing the water, we tied pieces of fishing line between two sticks, put the scorpions onto the fishing line and edged them along with our fingers to see whose scorpion would get to the other side first. I don't know how we knew scorpions had good balance. I know now that small pincers and a big tail mean the scorpion is poisonous – I cannot believe we did not incur any injuries.

I've since learned that fear is ingrained in us from such a young age. Unfortunately, the concept of destiny is not part of our educational conditioning. If we all knew that negative experiences only occur as part of our destiny, we would experience so much more joy. We restrict our activities and our capacity to love as a result of this ignorance. As children, scorpions had great entertainment value because we were unaware of their capabilities. We did not consider the possibility of being hurt; we simply enjoyed the experience.

My days were filled with fearless play until one critical day when I was six years old.

Somewhere inside of me, I knew that God must exist; although I did not know where, or how. While I never imagined I would ever see Him, I thought at least it should be possible to feel Him. Thoughts such as these would suddenly appear out of nowhere to occupy my mind. Lying next to my grandmother, I would fall asleep at night observing them dance in rhythm to the pulse of my heartbeat while infusing the blood flowing into my head with their mysterious enquiry.

On one of these nights, two significant thoughts floated into my awareness: 'What if all of this is just a thought in the mind of God, and what if, like a thought, at some point, we disappear?'

It filled me with wonder at the largeness of what God must be. Many nights I would fall asleep contemplating what He must be, where He must be, and what He must feel like.

SAMADHI

The watcher and the watched

One Friday night just before 7 pm, my father's youngest sister, Aletta, called for me to buy bread and milk from the shop for her. Walking along the untarred road on the way back, I approached the third avenue in a junction of four avenues.

The strangest feeling overcame me. Suddenly, I felt as if I could see not just in front of me, but all around me. I felt completely removed from my body.

I felt like water was being poured in reverse out of the cup that was my body. It seemed like I was everywhere – uncontained. Arriving back home, I held my hands up towards my aunt to hand over the bread and milk. I realised; I had completely lost the ability to speak.

Later, I recall laying on my back when a sound I did not recognise rang through me. It was not only in my head; it pervaded my entire body. As a six-year-old, it felt *so* huge, and I *so* small. I was engulfed by a larger sense of awareness. At times I felt like I was watching eyes watching me. The experience of being watched and the accompanying feeling of being understood was simultaneously both astounding and comforting. I became aware of standing before a giant void – the source of this sound.

This lasted for the next nineteen hours, starting at 8 pm that night. I remember it was Saturday and I did not have to be at pre-school.

When I did not wake up the next morning, my best friend's mother, my great-grandmother, and my neighbours were in an absolute panic. They felt no pulse in my body, nor breath flowing in or out of me. I occasionally felt someone touch my right hand and heard the distress of people trying to revive me. I was completely absorbed in the sound. I cannot say I felt weightless, but there were no borders – no barriers to my body or my awareness.

Aunty Makoti, my grandmother, and my great-grandmother thinking it dangerous to touch someone in such a state, were at a loss as to what they should do. Eventually, Aunty Makoti took the risk and rubbed my right arm, then force-fed me a protein drink.

Aunty Makoti's son Norman and I did everything together. Along with my grandmother, she raised me and played a pivotal role in ensuring I felt loved and taken care of. It was understandable that the voice I heard the clearest during all this was Aunty Makoti's.

I did not wake up until 3 pm the next day. I opened my eyes and there was no one in the room with me. I suspect they received confirmation that I was going to live otherwise why did they not call the mortuary? It is the most obvious thing to do if you think someone is dead. I vomited the pink and strawberry-flavoured stuff they force-fed me in their panic. Nothing inside of me was ever the same after this.

Silent questions

Following that experience, many questions appeared in my mind, all dealing with God – where He is, what He is, why He is, why I am, what is all this, and where do we go after this? All these questions arose but were never vocalised. I knew no one could ever answer them and I felt it was safer to keep my thoughts to myself.

I slowly moved towards Aunty Makoti and cousin Norman's house. Passing through the front door, it felt as if I was gliding rather than walking. The overpowering sound in my head had disappeared and It felt like I was seeing everything for the first time.

Years later, I asked Guruji about this incident. He told me that it was at this stage that he became aware of me – at six years old.

THE WATCHER

Duality

Nothing was ever the same, yet it took until I was sixteen to discover that the sound I heard from the void was the sacred sound of OM, the cosmic sound of creation.

My interest progressed from scorpion racing to watching. I found myself watching everything. Often, I would find myself alone, watching myself.

Questions that arose through this watching; particularly the question of Karma and cause and effect, I carried within me until I was twenty-three.

Being still, often daydreaming; I was very aware of the dual personality that was me. The me that knew what needed to be done and was always striving for certain outcomes, and the me that understood that I did not need to make decisions or do anything at all to make things happen. I experienced the difference between the two acutely.

I came to see how striving had become part of human nature. We are always desiring something or other, and in chasing those desires, we strive endlessly. We create grand scenarios in our minds about what a happy life would look like, and then we put our energies into creating this so-called happiness. Often we don't achieve the goals we set for ourselves; we don't get the things we desire. We then descend into suffering, feeling like failures and so continue to strive for other things. We are slaves to this striving and society is set up to perpetuate this quality of existence.

As a youngster, I was not able to articulate such wisdom. Instead, I felt the truth of it in my awareness as a watcher. Later, my Guru would provide the answer to this human quandary.

'Fortune' and 'misfortune'

I remember playing in the field of the primary school close to where I lived with my neighbour who was older than I when he asked me to squeeze the pimples on his back. Sitting on his back, squeezing his pimples, I experienced watching myself doing this from above. In that altered awareness, I became cognisant that some living beings were more fortunate in their life experiences than others. Yet another question entered my mind: 'What is it that determines fortune or misfortune?'

At this time, I was simply watching and learning. As children, we were responsible for placing our neighbour's chickens into the chicken coop at night. Of these twenty chickens, one was extremely weak and isolated. I remember thinking, 'What is the reason for a chicken of only a few months, to have such misfortune?'

One day, whilst putting them in the coop, a piece of metal we used to close the door from the outside fell on the neck of the chicken, injuring it. Not only did it endure similar misfortune, it looked as if it were in perpetual pain.

Nen and Sienna were our closest neighbours. With a table outside their kitchen window, they would often sit around the table drinking. One day, I jumped onto the table when I heard a commotion coming from their kitchen. To my horror, Nen was beating his wife as if she were a rag doll. He was much bigger and so much stronger than her. I immediately made the link between Sienna and the unfortunate chicken and pondered upon the similarity of their misfortune.

The violent imagery of Nen beating his wife remained in my mind for years. I wondered why Sienna did not try to defend herself. I knew Nen was a wonderful person when he was not drunk since I learned many things about dogs, chickens, and gardening from him. I also learned what I never wanted to become from him. I saw how he loved his chickens yet had no problem killing them most cruelly by wringing their necks.

My intense interest in people in terms of where they were on the continuum of fortune and misfortune, increased. Primary school presented me with hundreds more people to observe. It fascinated me to watch the interaction between teachers and their students. I had no real interest in scholarly learning yet managed to pass my grades convincingly. To me, learning occurred when watching people and nature. Nevertheless, the questions continued to germinate inside of me until many years later, when the answers would come from the infinite wisdom of my Guru.

The holy field of human experience

My Guru insisted His devotees read the Bhagavad Gita and listen carefully to His commentary. Through reading, and His subsequent discourse, I learned the human body and life itself is a holy field into which we are born. The world has a very specific purpose; and contains all the elements of experience that lead to our transformation.

The labels I placed on people's experience of life originate from a young mind unable to think beyond its human limitations. 'Fortune' and 'misfortune' are simply life experiences designed to help us learn and grow. These words, used in judgment imply that there are victims and perpetrators, when in fact there is only experience. When we take away human judgment, all we are left with are transformational experiences.

Where I observed the widely differing quality and circumstances of experience among the living, with their accompanying fluctuating emotions, my Guru and the Bhagavad Gita taught me to look upon them with equanimity. We are all destined to walk a very personal path, which some of us experience with greater intensity than others –º depending upon what we need for this lifetime. Now, my emotion upon seeing the 'unfortunate', is one of deep compassion and love. I know now that all experience is holy and it is one's personal path that determines everything.

MY GREAT-GRANDMOTHER

Selfless Service

It was during this time of keen observation that I recognized the amazing qualities my great-grandmother had. I noticed how other people were and saw a quality in her I did not see in them.

She was someone from whom I learned what selfless service was. I watched her actions and witnessed the effects of her service on those fortunate enough to be bathed in her light.

So many people were drawn to her. She was different and I was beginning to discover this difference. Even though we lived in two rooms, Granny never turned anyone away who needed a place to sleep or something to eat.

She was born in 1909. I remember her as an old woman collecting a government pension of R500 a month, which was the South African pension in 1982 for people of colour – a pittance by any standard.

Growing up with her was an incredible privilege. Years later, travelling back to Kokstad and seeing the place I called home, I remembered the garden that seemed to miraculously produce potatoes, carrots, green beans, radishes, and a giant rhubarb plant from which she made a memorable jam.

The eldest of nine children, though she was a great-grandmother, Christina Jansen-Booth was affectionately known to us children as Granny and to everyone else as Ous Gus. She headed up our family and steered us through the fluctuating weather of our lives. I watched her with great admiration.

I was the third generation to receive her loving attention and the feeling that all was well in the world. She played mentor to her much wealthier sisters, who I often saw in twos and threes seeking her counsel. Sometimes they even borrowed money from her, which made no sense to me.

I saw how much she meant to people by the community's response when she fell ill. People would flock to our house to see if she was ok, or if there was anything they could do. To me, she was superhuman. Capable of anything, yet quiet and content.

Sometimes my great-aunts Anne and Mavis would visit, but none of them were like my great-grandmother Christina. They were more similar to my grandmother Jessie, who smoked and drank. The bubble that my Grandmother Jessie was the only woman who partook in such vices soon burst.

Unconditional love

No matter what her daughter and sisters did, my great-grandmother Christina never judged them. She was ready to pick up the pieces for any mistake they made and nurtured their many children. When they had problems with their spouses, it was not unusual for four or five children to suddenly be dropped at her house. My mother told me that at one point ten people were living in those two rooms yet there never was the feeling of not having enough space or food. Granny Christina always provided the feeling of abundance.

Granny Christina did her best to pre-empt the difficulties that came the way of those in her care. When she couldn't prevent them, Granny would deal with the consequences without complaint. She never said, "I told you so". Hers was a silent steadfast love, patient to a fault in already difficult circumstances. Yet somehow, she managed to render flawless service to all of us.

The meaning of selfless service

My Guru taught me the meaning and implication of the selfless service I witnessed in my great-grandmother Christine, and He continues to demonstrate this in His service to His devotees.

In serving others with true sincerity, we turn away from the need to acquire experiences and things for ourselves.

Our selfish motives keep us bound to the world, to the endless cycle of lifetimes. By serving the individual self, we affirm the self. This constant affirmation keeps us tied to the world of self-serving values and actions. In contrast, by serving others, we let go of the 'I', and through our actions, do God's work.

My Guru taught me that there is nothing that God needs of us as individuals. When we serve, He does not *need* our services in and of themselves. When we think we are needed to fulfil certain activities, we are filled with self-importance.

Instead, through our Guru and His organisation, we are offered the opportunity to forget our desires and serve others in various ways. We benefit from this selfless service.

In serving and forgetting ourselves, we are closer to the Truth of who we really are. When we reach the point where we serve without the need for acknowledgement, for praise, to be noticed, to feel superior, or whatever other hidden selfish gains there are, then we live in God. We are part of God, no longer hypnotised by the material glamour of the outside world.

Granny Christina asked for nothing. I feel so grateful to have been born into her orbit. It was a great gift of love from God to have her as a role-model of selfless service.

MY GRANDMOTHER

Escaping life

My grandmother, Jessie Booth, was the youngest and most unencumbered of the children. I say unencumbered because she seemed to live the life she wanted on her terms. She led a wild life and often disappeared for long periods.

I remember waking up to Granny Christine in mid-conversation with a neighbour, telling them about her dream. She had a determined look on her face and was saying, "I had a dream of my husband, in which he said, 'You need to find my daughter'". Granny Christine's deceased husband was referring to my grandmother Jessie, who once again was away from home.

My grandmother Jessie played the horses and during this period had won a large amount of money. She was living in Ixopo at the time. Some of the young men from the track followed her after she secured her winnings assaulted her and stole the money she won. Grandmother Jessie was never the same after that experience.

My memories of Grandmother Jessie go as far back as when I was crawling. She was the only woman I knew who smoked and wore pants. She was tall, dark, and extremely strong-willed and demonstrated little affection to those around her.

I remember crawling without a nappy to the open wood stove oven. I put the cat inside the oven and closed the door. Immediately thereafter, a coal fell from the stove. I sat on it. I remember the pain, me crying and grandmother Jessie shouting at me. She was holding a cup of black tea and a cigarette in the other hand, wearing cerise nylon bell bottom pants. She watched this happening and did not stop me from putting the cat in the oven.

She took whichever man she wanted as a lover and when bored with him, let him go. I remember about three of them. They always seemed to love her more than she loved them. As well as smoking, she was also an avid drinker; her humour seemed to improve after a few drinks. She loved drinking iJuba, the traditional sorghum beer. Since she was more absent than present, I did not get the chance to know her, yet she taught me a lot about the human condition.

It would be so easy to judge someone like Grandmother Jessie. Her behaviour was not that of a dedicated family woman. She left the responsibility for her children to her mother, contributing little to their home life. She had little capacity for affection and treated the men in her life like disposable appendages.

Yet my Guru has taught me to look beyond the surface of what we see and experience. He taught me to have compassion for the pain that drives behaviour. Grandmother Jessie was lost. She'd lost sight of who she was and indulged in smoking and drinking to dull the pain.

So many of us are like my Grandmother Jessie. We are so lost to ourselves, that we search in the world to find that missing 'something'. When we don't find it, we use anything we can to hide from the pain. It's not just drugs or alcohol that we use. We might work, diet, eat or shop excessively. There are numerous ways in which we dull the pain.

When I think back on Grandmother Jessie and Great-Grandmother Christina, I see kaleidoscopic expressions of life in both of them. The light of selfless service, and the darkness of pain-filled self-absorption. It was all a mirror of my own experience of many lifetimes, and in experiencing their journeys, I was preparing for my own.

MY FATHER

Warmth and protection

Early childhood memories of my father left an indelible mark on my psyche. I had not reached my first birthday when I first felt his protection. My cousin Veronica and I were both asleep on the bed against the window. I remember a really loud sound as a stone came hurtling through the windowpane and glass fell in shards on both Veronica and I.

It turned out that Veronica's father, in a drunken rage, tried to get her mother's attention by throwing a stone from the road. Fortunately, the glass did not cut Veronica or me, but I recall with warm fondness my father's protective retaliation against this man.

I had cute baby teeth with a gap in the middle and was not allowed sweets. My treat was a Tropika drink and cheese and onion crisps once a week.

Even at three years old, there was an awareness that I was watching myself sitting on my father's shoulders thinking how cute I looked with a gap in my teeth!

I have fond memories of my father buying me ice cream, of sleeping in between my parents on the same bed, of the two of them kissing, and of watching them bake a chocolate cake together.

MY MOTHER

A force to be reckoned with

I was three months old when my mother started working at the hospital in Kokstad as a switchboard operator. Since she was the first woman of colour to work in that department, they built an office for her on her own, as it was illegal for her to share space with her white co-workers.

She was not allowed to use the toilet next to her office. The toilet designated for people of her racial group was five or six minutes away.

When she refused to use that toilet, the administration built her one that was more conveniently placed. Such was her determination and self-confidence in the face of appalling racism.

From her, I learned to value who I was and what I had to give, no matter the circumstances. In apartheid South Africa, my mother's movements were constrained by the laws of that time. People of her colour were treated as second-class citizens, and this had a debilitating impact on the psyche of millions of South Africans.

My mother did not allow what they thought of her to affect her. Instead of being defined by racist attitudes and behaviours or kowtowing to them, she transcended the world of ideas and operated from a place of deeper Truth. She was very aware of the value of her contributions. As a result, the people around her were compelled to give her what she deserved.

Know thyself!

Later, my Guru would teach me about the nature of the soul, and how it is separate from the body. The soul holds the Truth of who we are, but we forget this when we are engaged in the world of ideas and action. The soul's attention becomes fixated on the world and then the lines between the soul and the body become blurred in the mind. We begin to imagine that we *are* the body. It is only when we realise that the soul is who we are and is pure and untouched by anything in the world, that we realise that we have access to something higher and more profound. We can tap into something deeper; we can transcend the ideas of this world.

On some level, my mother knew this, although she did not articulate it in the way my Guru did.

Amusingly, to this day, in the New South Africa, that toilet still exists in Kokstad as a testament to her tenacious nature!

Fond memories

When I was five, my mother had the opportunity to work in a hospital in Pietermaritzburg. Since no plan included me, I was left to live with my Great-Grandmother Christina. I saw my mother sporadically after that, maybe two or three times a year. The memories I have of her from then and slightly before are a bit muddled.

I recall playing in the garden with one of the girls from next door, picking up small stones for some unknown reason. I found a stone small enough to put in my nose, so I did. When I tried to remove it, it would not come out. I went to my mother, who was visiting from Pietermaritzburg, looked up at her and pointed to my nose. I thought for sure she would shout at me. She did not. Instead, she smiled, bathed me, and held my hand on the way to the doctor's surgery to see what could be done about dislodging the stone in my nose.

Upon arrival, the doctor's assistant took a look at my nose, shook her head, patted my cheek, and disappeared. Suddenly I had a strong desire to sneeze. As I did, there was snot everywhere with the stone in the middle – I no longer needed to see the doctor!

From as far back as I can remember, I loved cats. I recall asking my mother to paint my face like a cat. On another occasion, I asked her to dress me up as a girl and take my photograph while I stood under a peach tree. I think the peach tree was in bloom.

I felt comfortable with my mother although I cannot say I felt the kind of bond I imagine other children at that age might have had with their mothers. Her distance from where we lived caused me to focus my attention on Granny Christina and my wild carefree life.

Irrespective, her presence in my life was significant. Like my Great-Grandmother Christina and Grandmother Jessie, my mother mirrored the nature of reality back to me, so that later I could look back to her example of the Truth about the nature of the soul.

MOVING TO PIETERMARITZBURG

Change

Moving to Pietermaritzburg at the age of nine was a clear indication to me that love and pain are two sides of the same coin. The great love that I felt for the countryside, for my friends, and for the wonderful memories of our unforgettable play, matched the degree to which I suffered when I had to leave. It was one of the most difficult periods I have ever experienced.

My mother decided to move me to live with her. Now that she had established a new life for herself, she wanted to take responsibility for me and offered to move my Great-Grandmother Christina too, but the old lady refused. She said there would be no one to fill her role in Kokstad.

The pain in my heart was so intense, I cried for days for a life that was no longer mine. I fantasised about my friends coming over the nearby hill to take me back with them. It never happened.

My emotional reaction to the pain was to refrain from loving anyone. My mother noticed this and called it 'the closing of my heart'.

I did not know it then, but my reaction was indicative of the human fear of change. A change in circumstances is a doorway to new experiences, but since we cannot know what is on the horizon, we cling to what we know instead. Even if what we know is making us unhappy. The closing of my heart was an attempt to block out new experiences, an effort to hold on to my childhood loves – my friends and my old home.

Much later, I would learn from my Guru that change is inevitable on this spiritual journey. No one gets to stay the same because transformation requires that we leave the old way of seeing ourselves behind.

A new school

My mother's life in Pietermaritzburg was not completely foreign to me, since I had visited her on several occasions after she remarried. I just really did not know how to feel about it, especially now that I was living here permanently.

The biggest problem for me was the feeling of boredom. There was no place to play outside. For someone like me who enjoyed the outdoors and nature, there was not much to do.

In time, my mother enrolled me in Raisethorpe Primary School where my language of instruction was no longer Afrikaans, but English. It was like existing in a completely different dimension. At first, I struggled, but it soon became easier to communicate.

Since I was so absorbed in the adjustment, I sometimes moved away from my 'watching' because the city was so big, loud, and overwhelming. What was clear was that I no longer carried a feeling of love within me. The pain of loss made me afraid to feel; I was reluctant to embrace others, and I became emotionally isolated.

The children in my class and the teacher were as welcoming as I was distant. In time, my reluctance to open my heart to others began to recede and I befriended Kerwin Ohlson. He became my very good friend and remained so for the rest of my time at primary school.

I always knew I was not a good note-taker. I was a listener, so more inclined to remember verbal instructions and visual methods of learning. This is how I navigated school.

High school

Time passed and my years at primary school ended. I moved to a high school close to home in a predominantly Indian area where I experienced a multitude of cultures.

Although my high school was about a seven-minute walk from my home, my stepdad always drove me.

I closely observed the buildings and the students as we waited for our school transfers to be confirmed. I felt things could be different here. I also noticed how comfortable I was not speaking to anyone. I simply enjoyed just watching.

The year I started high school was the very first year this Indian school had received students of other races. It was the New South Africa, the post-apartheid era, where people of different races were now mixing in every kind of social setting. I tried to find one other person who was the same race as me. There were only two others in the entire school.

High school was the place I realised I could choose who to associate with. The memories of my childhood adventures in the countryside were far away now. So was the heartache of not being where I wanted to be. I now had to navigate this new experience.

The friendships I made at this time happened so naturally. People just walked up to me and started talking. Hussein was the first. He was really impressed by my accent. It was an easy and natural relationship. I befriended Umang and Salim next. Although we were not in the same class, our friendship lasted for the duration of our time at high school.

The subjects that held my interest became very clear within the first few months of high school. I had no aptitude for mathematics, but I found languages, biology, and science quite easy to learn.

My teachers fascinated me and I built friendships with them. I especially liked my English and Afrikaans teachers and developed close relationships with them.

Searching for God

I found Rose, my English teacher, interesting because of the views she held about God. I still held the unspoken mystical questions hidden in my heart. I listened in the hope that somehow these questions would be answered.

Rose shared a different perspective than the one perpetuated at Sunday school. Fortunately, my parents were not particularly religious, so I was not forced to hold fast to any particular view. As long as my belief adhered to the Christian and not Jehovah's Witness doctrine, my parents were unfazed by any views I expressed. They never interfered, but sometimes asked questions.

In the beginning, it was an incredible feeling to attend the very small home-based church composed of family members and intellectuals. At times I found the information dry, yet I enjoyed the fact that it was more interesting and challenging than the Christianity followed by most people. However, I could not feel the presence of God during worship.

Friendship and laughter

The last three years of high school were my absolute favourite. I had fun and laughed a lot. It started in Standard 8 when I met people who presented a different perspective from what I was accustomed to.

I had never laughed so much in my life until I met Virginia. She told the most outrageous jokes and taught me how to relax since she thought I was quite serious about my 'God business'. We were from completely different cultures. Over those remaining years of high school, I learnt of the struggles faced by her and her family.

The following year, Brenda Duffy joined our class. She was the fourth person who looked like me in the school and an amazing storyteller who held our attention and brought more laughter into our lives.

Although Umang, Hussein and Salim were in a different class, we still kept really close. These five people brought a different quality to my experience. I could not have asked for better. Virginia was full of surprises. I think it was in Standard 9 when she suddenly started putting on weight, but we did not give it much thought. Everything continued as normal until the September holidays of that year. When we returned to school, Virginia looked different. I made some remarks about the change in her appearance. Without hesitation, she replied, "I had a baby." I could not believe it! We both burst out laughing and she continued to describe the excruciating pain of childbirth. She was so grateful for the conveniently placed school holiday. No one needed to know. We were amazed at how well she kept the secret.

In my final year of high school, I became aware of a skill I did not realise I had. Brenda Duffy who sat next to me, was sharing a story of her childhood in Ifafa, a small coastal resort town on the south coast of KwaZulu-Natal. I was listening intensely and asking questions. Suddenly, I heard the teacher address me loudly asking me to pay attention. I responded by telling him that I had heard the other three conversations that were happening simultaneously. He challenged me to repeat all three conversations – and so I did.

Almost all my oral examinations for English and Afrikaans were on topics related to spirituality or esoterica. It was clear that my focus on God never changed. I am so grateful to all the people who played a part. I have tried to reconnect with some of my friends and teachers. Unfortunately, the only person I managed to stay in contact with is Brenda who shares the same attention to detailed storytelling as she did when we were at school. Even though we do not connect often, when we do, we still roar with laughter at the absurdity of the antics of our youth.

THE ROADMAP TO GOD APPEARS

Restlessness

The last year of high school filled me with a sense of anxiety about the future. The idea of living an ordinary life was inexplicably terrifying to me. I could not imagine myself working at a job or attending university. As the year drew to an end, an uneasy restlessness swept over me.

It did not appear that anyone else was thinking in the same way, or asking the same existential questions that I was quietly asking myself. While my classmates engaged in a variety of worldly conversations about following certain professions and where they would live, the only topic that haunted me was that of God. I wanted to know more about Him, so I started reading what became my favourite book, The Larousse Encyclopaedia of Mythology.

The search for God continues

It was my constant companion at night as I explored how humans from antiquity to modernity related to God. It was the only information of this nature available to me, as my school library did not have an esoteric section and I did not know where to look for books of a similar genre in the town library.

God was the biggest feature in my mind. Other preoccupations came and went, but the need to know Him and feel His presence became my obsession.

The birth of my sister during that year marked a change in the religious nature of my parents as several circumstances began to mould their relationship with God. My stepdad became really sad after his job ended at the hospital where he had worked as an administrator for many years.

I learned his sadness was a form of clinical depression. It was during this period that he turned to God. Every night I heard him pray for change; pray for the feeling to pass – pray for understanding. His focus on God seemed to motivate my mother as she too turned to God during this time.

As my last year of school drew to an end, I met it with God in mind. He was all I wanted to pursue. I was uncertain as to how I would find Him, and I could not say too much to those around me – friends who had made more concrete plans.

This decision to find God was the beginning of my road to the feet of my Master. I know now that He was always patiently waiting and that it was He who had lit the flame of inquiry in my soul. He who had invited me to begin my journey to Him.

Not knowing where to start, after school ended, I found myself back in Kokstad.

DISCOVERING INTUITIVE ABILITIES

Seeing beyond the physical

My spiritual journey was to begin in earnest when in the first month back in Kokstad, I suddenly found my entire body covered in painful sores. I had no idea what caused them, yet I did not feel inclined to seek medical treatment.

Soon after, I discovered the ability to intuit people's lives. Often, clear pictures of people in their past and future would appear in my internal vision. Usually, these images were connected with big life events.

While talking to my friend Dean, I became aware that he would lose the use of his legs because I could see him in a wheelchair without the ability to walk. Since it was very difficult to relay this information to him, I could only tell him to be careful. Twenty years later, he was involved in a car crash that left him bound to a wheelchair for mobility.

Another friend learned about each of her pregnancies, as well as the gender of each child, from me – before she even conceived.

One day, I was walking alongside someone, when suddenly I said to her, "In a year's time you will give birth to twins, a girl and a boy." She laughed and said she had all the children she wanted. I said, "We will see." I met the twins ten years later when I delivered something to their home.

It was extraordinary to me. Word of this ability to foretell the future circulated in the small community of Kokstad. People responded to it with fascination, fear, and curiosity. A local businesswoman asked me to visit her place of business as she wanted to experience this for herself. Not long after, a friendship ensued between her family and I.

One day, a lady asked for a psychic reading. After I granted her wish, I told her I could not see anything in her future. She was plagued by so much hate, that she was constantly finding herself in conflict with others. I told her that she needed to apologise for the things she said to her husband. She was always telling him that he was so offensive to her, that she wished she were dead. I told her, "Be careful what you wish for."

This same woman went to a pub with a friend of mine when suddenly a soldier with an AK47 opened fire and shot her in the head. She died instantly.

HEALING MODALITIES

Reiki

It was during this time when I learnt of a teacher of healing who would be giving a course on the south coast of KwaZulu-Natal. I convinced my friends that it would be a good idea to learn such a skill. This is how I came to study the first level of the healing art of Reiki.

It was a fascinating journey which deepened my intuition and answered many questions I had about the mind-body relationship. The Reiki healing methodology originated in Japan and is administered by laying hands on the patient. Through the focused intent of the healer, energy flows from a 'universal' source, through the healer, to the patient.

Through my journey with Reiki healing, I discovered how all physical ailment has its root in something either mental or emotional or both, and reflects the ideas and thoughts we carry around with us.

Inner work

I progressed through the levels of Reiki, learning from different teachers and through this work, pieced together what I felt were the missing parts of myself. During this ten-year journey, I'd been involved in several painful relationships, in which I'd come face to face with my sense of inadequacy. Using my pain as a study, it was an amazing time of exploration.

Beyond Reiki

As my studies intensified, I developed modes of healing that superseded Reiki. I saw how everyone lives their life according to the limits imposed by the mind. I discovered the laws of karma and learned that each of us is not actually this body, instead, we are a soul that mistakenly identifies as a body. I linked this metaphysical wisdom to the mind-body incongruities that showed up as illness, and I saw how all this knowledge converged to express a story of the misery of the human condition.

The different teachers I met added to my growing range of skills that were each an important piece in the jigsaw of my development. It was an incredible time filled with many amazing experiences.

Travel is growth

I travelled all over South Africa acquiring different skills. While volunteering at an art gallery, I met someone who became very important to me.

An exhibition and artist-in-residence programme was being created for a very famous South African portraitist, Reshada Crouse. I met her work before I met her as I spent much of my time mounting her paintings.

I was amazed that somebody with such skill existed and that I had access to both her and her work. Having studied some of the works of the great masters of the Renaissance in high school, my opinion of her work was that it was on a par with theirs. I took a concentrated interest in her process and found an incredible person in Reshada.

We spoke while she painted, and we built the beginnings of a warm friendship. Towards the middle of her time at the artist-in-residence programme, she said, "One day you should come and visit me" and gave me her telephone number. I called her when her exhibition was over, and she welcomed me into her home and her life.

I learnt so many new things as I watched her work. She displayed such skill and talent, that I felt incredibly inspired by her devotion to her art. It was this dedication that gave me the courage to develop my skills further by travelling to cities in South Africa I had never visited before.

Travel opened my mind in ways I had not thought possible. In Cape Town, while in conversation with a teacher of flower essence therapy, I suddenly became aware of her entire body as if it were my own. I said to her, "I hope you don't mind if I tell you what I feel now...". Fortunately, she was open-minded and said, "Please do!"

I began to take her through all the things that were currently happening in her physical body in the smallest detail. She was so taken by this that she not only invited me into her practice in Cape Town but arranged for several people to experience the same psychic body exploration.

This gift of being able to know what was happening in the bodies of other people was yet another confirmation of how connected we all are. By transferring my awareness to her body, in some way her physical experience became mine. This human ability to transfer our consciousness and experience each other's feelings, emotions, and physical sensations, is testament to the fact that we are not this body.

Joanna Castle was a traditional Reiki Master and offered me the opportunity to begin my Reiki master's course. She was also a natural perfumer, a modality I later practised myself.

Pain has a purpose

I did not just learn about healing, I also learnt why I needed healing. Understanding my pain, confusion, and fear, and how that played out in my different behaviours of unappreciation, impatience, and unkindness helped me to develop appreciation and kindness.

I learnt the importance of difficulty and struggle, because only through pain do we see who we truly are, and so only then do we make the effort to have a different experience.

Where we place our attention counts

During this time, I realised that having a little and having a lot are the same. This is because happiness is not found in things. We think it is but find out soon enough that this is not true. Ultimately, the only determining factor as to whether I am content or not is based on which thoughts I focus my attention on. If I have little, I can choose to focus on scarcity, on those thoughts that constantly tell me what I should have, but don't. Or I can choose to focus on what I *do* have. In other words, I can show gratitude for what exists in my life. We always have *something*, even if it's not what we were expecting.

This life experience taught me to appreciate the value of people. I experienced the kindness and welcoming of so many wonderful people. I learnt the importance of friendship, respect, and trust. At the heart of all of this was the presence of God.

My wish to see the world from a different perspective was fulfilled. The right people always arrive at the right time. Looking at it from where I am now, it was like they were always waiting. I see my Guru's calling card in the network of people who have become an important part of my life.

MEETING A YOUNG MAURITIAN SAINT

And so it begins

By the early 2000s, I was spending more time in Johannesburg. I was usually at the house of my friend Reshada, who on one of those occasions told me of a place called Vision Lodge, a centre for healing and therapeutic massage. I took the location from her and found my way there.

I was met by the owner, Vanessa Kaye. I provided details about my history in the healing field, and enquired whether it would be possible to practise at her establishment. She asked for a demonstration. I remember sitting on one of the benches in the garden and my instinct was to put my hand on her lower back where I sensed she was experiencing pain. After about seven minutes I removed my hand. She was amazed that there was no longer any pain.

I started practising at Vision Lodge the very next day. To begin with, she made calls to her clientele informing them of the arrival of a new therapist, then showed me the different treatment rooms spread across one of the most beautiful gardens I had ever seen. Soon, I was treating a rapidly increasing number of clients. It was such an incredible period. I felt privileged to meet people from every conceivable background.

The value of friendship

A year and a half later, Vanessa and I had developed a really good friendship when she announced to all of her staff that she had stage 4 breast cancer. She lived a very healthy life, was an integrated massage teacher, and was a truly grounded person. She'd done everything right physically, yet she still contracted cancer.

The most natural response from me was just to be there for her and to help her move through this time, doing whatever I could to make her comfortable. I watched the pain, sometimes with anger and frustration.

Seeing the slow process of her recovery, I watched as her friends rallied around her, giving her all the support she needed. I had a direct experience of the value of friendship. When she had fully recovered, she spent some time away from Vision Lodge.

An auspicious email

A friend of Vanessa's who was house-sitting the centre with me received an email inviting her to meet a young Mauritian saint. I walked into the office as the email was being read to the secretary. I asked where the event was and if I could accompany her. It was being held at the Ishta School of Yoga, a five-minute walk from Vision Lodge. There was no further information about the

Mauritian saint or what He would be doing. This was two weeks before the event. Life continued as normal, then the day of the event arrived.

Seeing Him for the first time

It was a cold afternoon in June when I arrived at the Ishta School of Yoga, intrigued at the prospect of meeting someone who was described as a "young Mauritian saint". Walking into the room, I encountered many people I knew from the healing world. Everybody was either seated on the floor or on chairs facing the front of the room, where there was a stage, arranged so that when He sat, His feet could touch the ground.

I sat in the centre of the room and greeted people but did not indulge in conversation. We waited. I closed my eyes. One hour passed, then another, and then another. My attention drifted in and out. I knew He'd arrived when suddenly the room fell silent.

I opened my eyes as He was preparing to take His seat. My first thought was, "I know Him". I suddenly realised that it was His face I'd seen in my dreams every night since the email arrived inviting my colleague to the event. The invitation did not include a photograph of Him. I recalled the dreams were mainly conversations.

I moved to a place where I could see Him clearly as He started singing several bhajans for Shirdi Sai Baba.

Behind him, was a large photograph of Baba. Then He proceeded to give what I now know as 'Darshan'. I watched as He, one by one, touched the front and back of each person's head. His thumb was on the third eye and his middle three fingers at the back and nape of the neck. As He touched people's heads in this way, I saw Him looking at them in a manner that appeared slightly out of the ordinary to me. Naturally, I imagined He was looking into peoples' eyes, but then I saw He was not; He was looking beyond the physical, at something which could not be seen.

My first Darshan

The love in His eyes felt extraordinary to witness since all of us there were strangers to Him. I later discovered that no one was a 'stranger'. He knew every soul in that room and was familiar with the paths we had taken. In those days, my limited mind could not find any reason for Him to pour such love into each person who sat before Him. I saw how His commitment did not change irrespective of what the person looked like. There was no judgment in His eyes as He gave this love equally to everyone.

About halfway through the evening, I joined the queue to receive His gentle touch and embrace. When my turn arrived, I kneeled in front of Him, looking into His eyes. He looked at me and then embraced me. I felt His heart beating under His skin.

Afterwards, I moved to a place where I could observe Him more closely. As I watched, I observed the suspension of breath for exactly seven minutes. I read about this form of advanced yoga but never thought it was possible. I noticed that His love appeared to increase with the suspension of breath. His body became still, and each movement effortless.

My service to Him begins

My first instinct after this evening was to share this encounter with as many people as possible. As this remarkable Mauritian saint would be there again the following evening, I telephoned my friends, as well as my clients from Vision Lodge, and urged them to experience this beautiful flow of love.

I could hardly wait to see Him again. I observed His actions once again. My friends and clients were impressed by how He remained so calm and still despite sitting for hours. They commented on His beauty and serenity, and how the entire room was enveloped with His almost palpable love.

I learnt who arranged this event and found myself sitting right behind her. All I said to her was thank you. Thank you for providing the opportunity to witness such magnificence. After three days of Darshan, the event ended.

I tried to contact the person who had arranged the Darshan. I knew He was still with her, that she was serving Him in some capacity. After telephoning to ask if I could assist, she was unavailable to take my call. She was in the middle of learning a bhajan with Guruji. I could hear His voice in the background teaching them the bhajan.

I wanted to be in His presence, but it was not the time. However, the seed was planted. I felt compelled to learn more about Him.

CONNECTING WITH THE MAURITIAN SAINT

Moving into my Hindu identity

Being in His presence for three days impacted my approach to healing. From watching Him, I was inspired to focus on a simpler way. Using His example, I started to apply one of the healing modalities of Reiki which requires focusing on the place needing healing without the need for touch.

This required focused intention and a quiet mind. I experimented with holding the person in a space of love. I then learnt that this energy could be transferred to any part of the body; all it required was intent and focus.

As I worked with this energy, I began to realize a need for a commitment of a different kind. I wanted to become a Hindu. Something was happening I did not understand. The healing energy I was directing to others was revealing who I was to become.

While visiting friends in Pietermaritzburg, I attended a Shri Bhagavatam Katar and asked if it was possible to undergo a 'conversion' ceremony. Technically, no such conversion ceremony existed, but there was a way for those who left Hinduism to return to the religion. The priest agreed to perform this ceremony for me.

He performed a fire ceremony and then invited me to stand in front of the main altar to choose the deity I felt most attracted to. He mentioned several but I already knew I would choose Shiva. The priest started to recite some mantras and I felt a stream of energy in the space between my eyes. My entire forehead was pulsating and vibrating with this energy. I felt connected to an even greater stream – a source of energy that would always flow through me.

Of course, I now realise that I was never disconnected from this source. None of us are. We are part of that great source of love – God. Now, my awareness was refocused. As long as I stayed true to that focus, that love would direct my path.

Time passed and the quality of my healing work changed for the better.

Acknowledgement from Him

My work was punctuated by visits to the Mauritian saint whenever possible. I would attend events, receive Darshan, and speak about Him to various groups of people to explain the meaning of Darshan. I did not have any form of personal relationship with Him. He did not know me very well. I was just there, seeking Him, waiting for something I could not define. Talking about Him to others helped connect me to Him.

An event of great significance to me was a Darshan given on MahaShivaratri in 2002 where miraculous events occurred. It was the first time He acknowledged me and was the moment my relationship with Him developed into something deeper.

Appearing at the Ishwara Kovil in Lenasia South, the Mauritian saint, whom I now call 'Guruji', was giving Darshans while lingams were coming out of His mouth. In absolute awe, I remember thinking how painful this must have been.

I attended this Darshan with a friend from the Ishta School of Yoga who was several people behind me in the queue. I approached Guruji and then kneeled in front of Him. He looked at me, said my name and asked how I was. My first reaction was to recall if I had given my name to anyone because I had not spoken to anyone or written my name in any of the registration books. I tried to establish if perhaps, my friend had told Him my name. During my mind's scrabbling, He smiled and tried to make conversation, while all I could think about were the almost 1,000 people still waiting in the queue.

Baffled, I stood up and walked away. Later, this encounter would be one I would replay in my mind, knowing that by His enquiry, he was indicating I belonged to Him.

Shortly after, my friend and I tried to leave and spent the better part of two hours trying. Even though we were familiar with the area, we just could not find the exit routes and found ourselves driving around in circles – lost. Four years later in conversation with Guruji He asked: "Remember the time we first met? You got lost when you were leaving, right?" I said yes. He replied, "That is because I was not finished speaking to you."

Connection

The days following this Darshan became the defining moments of my spiritual journey. Once, while standing in the kitchen preparing lunch, I heard Guruji's voice gently call my name repeatedly in my right ear. I was more focused on His voice than on what He was trying to say. Hearing Him filled me with deep love and yearning for Him. I knew Guruji was still in South Africa.

The next morning, I had the same experience. This time, it was a name and a surname coupled with the feeling of great urgency. I felt He was saying, "You did not understand previously, I hope you get it this time."

My immediate impulse was to call the number on the flyer distributed at Darshan. After a few rings, Hilde Light answered. She sounded really tired and a little ill. I found myself saying to this woman I hardly knew, "I need to know who He is, and how I can serve Him." I recounted my experience with Guruji a few days previously and how I felt about His presence. I wanted her to understand where this outpouring was coming from.

In turn, she explained how exhausted she was. Guruji had been in South Africa for over a week and stayed a few days in her home. Being the gracious host, she had not slept more than two hours a day since He arrived, so all she wanted to do was rest. I explained that I understood and would not take much of her time, but that I had to follow through with this.

We spoke at her home for about an hour, during which she shared her experience with Guruji. Then, she took me into her bedroom where Guruji had made a vibhuti manifestation just the day before.

He called her to say, "Hilda your room is a mess!" She replied, "Yes, your stuff is everywhere." He then countered, "No, not that mess ... this mess!" She peered into the room where she made a small altar on a chest of drawers against the wall. All the pictures of saints and deities were covered in vibhuti. There was also a huge cross of vibhuti on the wall. Vibhuti was coming out of the ceiling above the altar. Later, she noticed all the small pictures of deities stuck around the room were giving vibhuti too. She had a framed photograph of Shirdi Sai Baba above her headboard and when she slept, vibhuti fell on her face.

The manifestation of vibhuti was a wonderful expression of His love. But vibhuti was not what I was seeking. I wanted to know Him. He was what I was seeking.

Rebirthing

I found Hilde's work as a rebirther very interesting and saw it as an opportunity to deal with the pain and trauma I experienced within my relationships.

With this work, the emotions that surfaced were sometimes so overwhelming, it was difficult to breathe my way through certain ideas and thoughts that caused me pain.

I saw that healing occurred in proportion to the degree of my willingness to let go of how I felt about the people involved. Guruji's connection to this process was very clear and I knew He had sent me here to prepare for the steps that were to follow in my life.

Work on myself intensified and allowed me to be more available to others. I learned how everything is affected by how I view the past and future and that I could choose the way I see that past and accept it for the gift it is to me, or I can remain in a prison of pain.

I was astonished at how something as simple as connected breath could bring such transformation. My interest in handheld healing modalities grew and I learned several more techniques over the next year.

ORGANISING DARSHAN FOR GURUJI

A new challenge

I was the only one able to arrange the Darshan in Durban because I was the only one with time to do it. Ajit Haridas helped me. We did all the organising from his home and he graciously drove me me wherever I needed to go.

A few days before Guruji's arrival, Ajit and I met at the family home where we arranged for Guruji to stay. Everything was planned in detail, including meals and accommodation. Hilda, who was now responsible for coordinating all His events in South Africa, travelled with Him.

We arrived at the airport to fetch Guruji in the late afternoon. As He approached me, a headache began to form. It was the first headache I experienced as an adult. He looked at me and asked: "Where is your black shirt? You are not wearing it today." I looked at Him and said, "It is not a uniform, nor weather to wear silk or black." He smiled and we approached the waiting car.

We arrived at our destination, which was a really large double-story house. He placed His right foot in the doorway, took a step, stopped, and asked, "Whose idea was it for me to stay here?" Then He closed His eyes and said, "Oh I see now." He knew exactly whose suggestion it was and also what instructions had been given to the people hosting Him.

During the time we spent together over those two days, His behaviour towards me seemed familiar. During the evening, He wanted to sing some bhajans and asked me to sing the invocation prayers for Ganesha. I was particularly taken with His absolute self-confidence. I could not detect even the faintest self-doubt.

Learning from the Guru

Usually, people came to see Him during mealtimes. At one of those meals, while certain people were enquiring what He could do to change their lives for the better, He raised His head and said, "I cannot be bought" and continued eating. To this day, I see this in many of the people who follow Him. They view Him as a wish-fulfilling tree. In going to the Temple and performing certain sadhanas, they are bargaining with God; they want something in return for their devotion. They fail to understand that He is here to help them to Self-realise, and eventually God-realize. What they want is for Him to fix their lives without making any effort to transform themselves.

It was during this trip that Dr Jeevren Reddy promised Guruji that he would make a temple for Him. This is now becoming a reality as Shri Vishwananda Nilaya. Guruji sowed the seeds that would grow much later. It shows me that He is both omniscient and omnipotent. Nothing happens by accident. He plans everything.

The following day, the planned visit to see Swami Sachidananda occurred in the high humidity and excessive heat of Durban. Guruji exited His room wearing a red raw silk robe. I wondered how He would manage out there in the elements.

We arrived and Swami Sachidananda was there to greet us. After the formalities, Swami asked Guruji; "Which organisation do you belong to?" Guruji replied, "My own." Swami Sachidananda reached into His dhoti and handed over an envelope of dakshina to Guruji. Guruji looked at me and I understood that I should take it.

The holy gift of a ring

It had only been two days since He arrived, and the intensity of my headache had increased. The desire to have a ring like the one He made for Hilda consumed me, although I did not say anything to Him. I was holding it in my expectations.

We returned to where He was staying. As He ascended the stairs, I looked at Him from below. He said, "Come." When we reached the top of the stairs, He turned to me, shook His head, and looked at me as if to say, "Poor you…" Then He turned His right hand and showed me a ring, just like Hilda's, except for a few modifications. I hugged Him tightly. He laughed, "You are squeezing me, you are squeezing me!"

Later that evening, while talking to Hilda and showing her the ring, I told her of my headache. Guruji was standing on the other side of the room. There was no way He could have heard what I was saying. Suddenly He said, "That sometimes happens when people are in my presence." That was the end of the headache. It disappeared instantly.

Shortly after Guruji's visit, I met with Hilde, who told me that Guruji asked that we meet every two weeks to sing and to share stories in Satsang. This was the beginning of even greater things to come.

GURUJI MANIFESTS GANESHA

Answering His request

We continued the Satsangs as per Guruji's instruction. In the beginning, there were only three of us; Lorraine, now Kalindi; Hilda, now Driti; and I. We met every other Thursday in Kalindi's house in Hyde Park, Johannesburg, and spent an hour or more together, keeping the picture of Guruji at the centre of our focus. We built a small altar in the lounge where we celebrated Guruji's birthday.

Occasionally, a few more people would join. It was during one of these Satsangs when I heard of Guruji's plan to travel to Johannesburg and that I would have to arrange the next Darshan.

We met and planned exactly what to do – which hall to use, what the stage arrangements should be and other technical logistics.

I was relieved when Ajit agreed to travel from Durban to help with the logistics a few days before Guruji's arrival. The Darshan was advertised in several magazines and also spread by word of mouth by people who attended previous Darshans. It was very exciting. Although there were several more people in the Satsang group, they were not regular attendants. Each time Guruji visited, the number of followers increased. New people joined – some of them stayed, some drifted away.

Ganesha arrives

On the day of Guruji's arrival, we headed to the airport with great excitement. He stayed at Kalindi's house as the Darshan was in the nearby suburb of Bryanston. Guruji and I had not spent any time together except for our encounter in Durban on His previous visit. In our conversation at the airport, as we walked towards the car, He approached me, then asked: "You know the Ganesha you gave me? I really like Him. I keep Him on my personal altar." He then paused and said, "Remind me and I will manifest one for you."

My excitement ran rampant as I imagined when and where He would manifest it. I wanted to spend as much time with Him as possible. A newly manifested Ganesha murti would be an additional accomplishment.

It was during this visit that I discovered several ways to observe and change the flow of thoughts. At Kalindi's home, Guruji freshened up and decided to lead a yagna. During lunch, I was most amused to see Him eat pizza with a fork and knife by cutting it into little squares. I had never seen anyone do that. Seeing us languishing in His presence, He said to Ajit Haridas and I, "You need to hurry...Darshan is tonight and there is a lot to do." Reluctantly, we left.

I thought everything was set when I looked at the chair on the stage. It had no cover. It was a really old sofa that Guruji liked because it was comfortable. I remember the house I stayed in had satin sheets, so I ran back and covered the chair with a sheet. Three minutes later, Guruji appeared on stage and Darshan began.

I had already reminded Guruji about the manifestation of Ganesha twice and now He was leaving for the airport in Johannesburg to fly out to Mauritius the next morning. I was not invited to accompany Him as there was a lot of cleaning to do after Darshan.

I thought I would ask Him one more time. Even before the question came out of my mouth, He answered, "If you ask me one more time it will not come."

All my pent-up expectations became acceptance. I understood I can exert no control over what and when things happen. Irrespective of how much I push and nag, things happen in their own time.

It was a long day, and it was now too late to go home, so I stayed with Ajit Haridas at his niece's home in Midrand. At about 7am, my telephone rang. It was Umvati calling to say that Guruji was looking for me and I should call Him on His hosts' telephone.

When I made contact, He was on the way to the airport with his hosts. He said, "What it was I promised you, I am sending now to the house where I was staying. Go there in the afternoon to collect it."

I was shocked and surprised, wondering how He would manifest Ganesha while in traffic!

In the room where Guruji slept, there was a tray in which vibhuti had suddenly started materialising. Before He and the hosts had all piled into the car, He stood before the tray and instructed His hosts to let the vibhuti materialise for eleven days, then give half to a friend of Guruji and the other half to people who were sick. Then they all left the room and the house together.

After my conversation with Guruji, I arrived back at the house just as the host family were returning from the airport. To our surprise, when we entered His room, in the middle of the tray where the vibhuti was growing, was a small vigraha of Ganesha embracing the Shiva lingam.

He told me how to give blessings to people with Ganesha and said they should donate to charity after having received the blessing. A year later, when Guruji returned to South Africa, He asked to see Ganesha since He had only imagined Him in His mind and had not actually seen Him.

The Sangha grows

During this time, Guruji made His appearance felt through the Satsangs we were now having every other week in Kalindi's home in Hyde Park.

On his first trips to South Africa, there were no devotees. However, on subsequent trips, different people became increasingly connected to Guruji and became an integral part of His work in South Africa. It was only after some time we realised that all of us were present at the very first Darshan at the Ishta School of Yoga. Of course, we had no way of knowing this since we did not know each other. One by one, I met these people in scenarios unconnected to Guruji, only to find we had Him in common.

MATLAPENG

The Guru/disciple relationship

In my journey through life, I have gained much insight into the nature of the Guru/disciple relationship. I learnt that we do not meet Him until we are ready, and it is the trajectory of our lives which prepares us for this first meeting. On the road to Him, we search, we question, and we venture into new territories of life that transform us in different ways. By the time He appears, our minds are ready for the challenge His presence brings.

Even after that first meeting, He prepares us for different levels of relationship with Him. Whether we live in His Ashram or the world, He creates situations that challenge our perceptions of ourselves, our perceptions of the world, and Him. I desperately wanted His company. I wanted to be around Him, to serve. He knew I had much work to do before our relationship could develop into something deeper.

Preparation

In 2005, I heard a follower of Guruji's would be taking Brahmachari initiation at the Ashram He recently opened in Stefanshof, Germany. I was intrigued. I wanted to be closer to Guruji, and I too wanted to take initiation.

I tried several times to reach out to Guruji after I received this news but could not contact Him. I then called the person who was to be initiated, who told me Guruji was right there in front of him but did not want to speak with me.

Disappointed that He would not engage, I prayed for guidance as to where I should go now, and my prayer was to be answered most unexpectedly.

At that time, I was housesitting for my friend, Golchin, who was in France for several months. While there, I received a visitor, a man called Derek, who had been to see Mother Moon, a Native American storyteller and Seer I met several months before. He told me he posed a question to her she was unable to answer so she gave him my name and address. Fortunately, I was able to give him what he needed in terms of answers, and he began a series of healing sessions with me.

Derek followed the teachings of a group called the Wing Makers. During one of our healing sessions, he suddenly stood up and asked if I had just rung a bell. He heard one sound quite clearly. I replied, "Do you actually see a bell?" and he said, "No, but it's very important. Yesterday while reading the teachings of the Wing Makers, I read a line that said when you hear the sound of bells you will know you are proceeding in the right direction." Naturally, he was shocked when just one day after reading the teachings, he heard bells.

I told him of an upcoming workshop I was to participate in at Matlapeng, a mountain retreat outside Johannesburg. This workshop would challenge the way we think, and hopefully help free us from some limiting perceptions. After Guruji rejected my phone call, I felt the need for further growth.

Derek agreed to accompany me since he was following the guidance of the bell.

The same time I committed to that workshop; I received a message from the person to be initiated in Germany. He informed me that Guruji had given permission for me to come to Mauritius that year. I was elated because I knew this trip meant initiation into Brahmachari. I was compelled to follow this path. Remarkably, this trip was scheduled directly after the Matlapeng retreat.

Confronting the mind's limitations

We headed to Matlapeng, a rustic resort tucked away in kilometres of mountainous bush country, for the weekend course, designed to be the first in a series.

We were to participate in an exercise where Yasmin our facilitator presented the notion that we were pure creative beings, capable of manifesting anything. The fact that we were unable to manifest, was because we were polluted by beliefs that rendered us powerless. For a direct experience of this truth, Yasmin suggested we undergo a series of exercises.

In one of those exercises, we were to find a packet of potato chips and a bottle of water hidden within a three-kilometre radius.

Yasmin gave us a technique that helped us to focus entirely on the mental images of the potato crisps and the water. We were not to entertain any thoughts that arose when forming those images, because those thoughts were likely to be negative and influence our success in finding our targeted items.

With the image of water and potato chips in mind, we headed out into the bush. Having been given only half an hour, we came back empty handed. Yasmin looked at us with great disappointment at our inability to challenge any thoughts of 'I cannot' or 'I will not' or 'it is impossible'. She made us refocus and sent us back to repeat the exercise. With this rebuke and greater determination, we found the packet of chips hidden in the branches of a tree within five minutes. It proved what we were capable of, but unfortunately also proved what held us back, and how powerful our limiting beliefs are.

But we had to find the water, too. All three people in my group each focused intensely, heartened by our previous success. At first, we stumbled all over the place trying to focus, but constantly tripped ourselves up by thinking negative thoughts. Finally, when I had a grip on my focus, I looked down and saw a pipe with a tap. I opened the tap and water came streaming out. However, this was not the water we were looking for.

I said to my teammates: "Let us focus together. You grant me the energy and let me be the instrument for finding the water." We knew we had to be specific about the water we were searching for. It was a plastic bottle of mountain water, the kind you buy at the supermarket. We set off once again.

As I walked, my mind began to tell me how ridiculous I was, that even though I had been in this game for so long, I could not even find a bottle of water. Despite this, I kept trying to bring my thoughts back to the water even though my mind kept exploding with doubt and insults. I had to stop, refocus and continue on several occasions.

Finally, as I walked with a clear focus, allowing myself to be drawn to it, I looked down and suddenly there was the bottle, concealed by grass. I noticed there was no excitement or joy at finding it. I realised that this was not magic. It was a natural ability, hidden by limited thinking. I simply reached down and picked it up.

Exercises like these added yet another dimension to my understanding of the mind. The minefield of negative thoughts that kept us in mental slavery is not a trustworthy source of information. I realised that if I was to join my Guru through this initiation ceremony, I would have to navigate through a myriad of ideas that would try to stop me from moving forward.

The next exercise was to use our ability to send mental impulses. Each team consisted of two people. One had to hide and only by sending a mental message could they find the other again. Again, the mental impulse that we sent out had to be pure and unwavering.

My group had three people. I was the first to hide. From beneath the building, I sent the message, "I am here. I am here." I attracted everything; insects, dogs, other people, but not my team!

At one point, every one of my team members converged in the area I was hiding, but they were so in awe at seeing each other, they lost their focus and never bent down to discover my hiding place. They reluctantly returned to the starting point for their fourth attempt. Out of the numerous hiding spots available in the three-kilometre radius, they finally found me.

The next day, when one of them had to hide, I somehow knew where they were going before they did. My senses were so honed, that I found them within a few minutes.

Set to go

The next process was called 'the Hall of Mirrors' and consisted of a room with hundreds of cards posted on a wall. Messages were written only on the sides of the cards facing the wall.

Upon entering the room, we were to focus on our goals in the way that Yasmin had taught us. By lifting the cards with this mental focus, we would receive a message relating to the obstacles or beliefs preventing us from achieving our goals. Once we understood what was being said on those cards, and after spending time meditating on the messages, we entered the Hall of Mirrors again, and this time some of us discovered through subsequent messages that we had transcended certain obstacles. This final exercise cleared the way for my upcoming meeting with Guruji. I saw what was in my way and contemplated the issue deeply. I completed the entire process knowing I would take Brahmachari.

The work I did at Matlapeng was intense and filled me with the conviction that there was no other way for me but to be in His presence. The remaining time at Matlapeng provided even further validation.

Dreams come true

When I told Yasmin, she said she was worried about me 'giving my power over' to a Guru. I laughed at her, pointing out the power of her limited mind to alarm her in this way. She was adamant about saving me from myself! As it happened, she transcended her fears and became one of those devotees who surrendered everything to Guruji. Today, we look back in amusement at the way she responded to our Guruji!

As we left Matlapeng, I turned to Derek and said, "I am going to Mauritius on Thursday to spend time with Guruji, will you come with me?"

He looked back at me and said, "I am eighty percent sure I will be coming." I had been saving for this trip and made a booking with South African Airways that I would pay for on the day of the flight.

That night I was told in my dream that Derek was to pay for my flight. I wondered how I could ever relay such a message to him. As soon as I woke up, I phoned Yasmin and told her the dream I had. Her answer was simple; I had to tell him. I was so disturbed by this. I put the phone down on her and it rang two seconds later. It was Derek. He said he was going to the South African Airways offices in Rosebank to book His ticket and extended an invitation to join him. As I was about to pay for my ticket, Derek stopped me and paid for both of us without thinking twice. I asked him, "Why are you doing this?" He just smiled at me and said, "It's the least I can do for all you have done for me over these past weeks."

BRAHMACHARI INITIATION

Arrival

Thursday morning arrived and there was much excitement. Derek and I were at the airport, and I could not believe I was going to spend time with Guruji in his home country.

About halfway into the journey, I turned towards Derek and asked him, "What would you do if He asked you to become a monk as well?" He laughed and said, "Then I'd better eat my last beef stroganoff and drink my last whisky!"

As we cleared passport control in Mauritius, it suddenly occurred to me that I had not asked Guruji if Derek could also be there. I panicked. I felt mortified at the thought of Guruji's possible disapproval. After collecting our bags and exiting the airport building, we found the person who had just recently been initiated in Germany waiting for us.

My heart was in my mouth as this man looked at Derek and then asked me, "Did you ask Guruji if he could come?" And when I said no, he replied, "Well you had better try and get hold of Guruji." He made a big deal of it. I panicked further when upon reaching the centre, it was clear there was no way to get hold of

Guruji as He was travelling in India. All we could do was wait to hear what Guruji would have to say.

Time with Guruji

There were many people in the centre from all over the world. People from the UK, Germany, several other European countries, and Russia. They all came to spend time with Guruji. I spent those few days getting to know everyone, sharing responsibilities, deciding how to go about buying food, how to participate in cooking, cleaning, etc.

About three days after we arrived, Guruji appeared. It is difficult to describe the feeling I had after waiting so long to be in His presence. I missed Him and constantly yearned for His company. To my mind, His Darshan visits to South Africa were too few and far between.

On one of the first days after He arrived, I was seated on a small chair in the temple dedicated to Shirdi Sai Baba. Guruji entered. I automatically vacated the chair to give Him a place to sit. He asked if I was happy to be there. I replied, "Yes I am." It was so discomforting not knowing what formalities to use in such a setting. I simply did that which came naturally to me.

I did want to spend time with Him, but it was clear that it would be on His terms.

I soon realised this trip would not just be about basking in His light. He wanted to give us something far more profound than just spiritual niceties, but that gift would come at a cost to the ego.

A week into our stay, we made our first trip to the beach. Guruji was in the water for more than an hour and a half. I remained on the beach watching everyone swim and ensuring everyone's personal belongings were safe. After about two hours, Guruji waded out of the water towards the opposite end of the beach.

Walking behind Him I noticed an incredible fragrance wafting from His body. I ran to ask Him about the fragrance and why it remained so strong after swimming in the ocean. From the little I knew about perfume at the time, I knew that ozone in seawater cancels most fragrances.

He looked at me, smiled and said, "I am not wearing any perfume. From my elbow to my wrist and my knee to my ankle this fragrance emits." I looked at Him with absolute disbelief. I took His right arm and started to scratch the inside of His forearm. The fragrance increased, and somehow, I felt an overwhelming feeling of love. Standing there on the beach, I felt compelled to tell Him, "I love you and I surrender myself completely to you."

Empty words

He looked at me and said, "What did you say?" I said it again, and this time, He asked if I would say it in front of a witness. I agreed although I was a little taken aback at this request. He called the new Brahmachari initiate to witness my declaration and I repeated; "I love you and I surrender myself completely to you."

The events that followed made me realise I did not have a real understanding of what surrender meant. I knew it was a profound state of mind, and I liked the idea of saying it to this Guru that I loved. I thought that by saying it, I would somehow achieve it. After I said it for a third time in front of the witness, Guruji looked at me and said very ominously, "We shall see."

Testing times

A day later, I was sitting again in the Shirdi Sai Mandir when Guruji came in, and again we swapped seats. He looked at me and said, "You will become Brahmachari. The ceremony is next week." Something erupted within me, an explosion of love, of doubt, of fear of the implications of such a vow.

One day when walking down the passage from the kitchen towards the exit, we met. I was walking in the opposite direction. The space was quite narrow, and I accidentally brushed my left arm against Him. He turned around, looked at me and said, "Don't touch me."

This heightened the discomfort, anger, and frustration I was already feeling. I was accustomed to looking at my emotions, yet I could not locate a root cause for what I felt. What I did know is that I needed to address this with Him. I asked Him several times if it would be possible. He replied with vague statements like, 'Maybe later', or 'Let's see'. He was rather nonchalant and non-committal.

I was left alone with what I was feeling and went from speaking, interacting, and laughing with everybody, to sitting in front of the fish tank, reading the one thousand names of the Goddess in total solitude. At night while sleeping I would dream of Him, and in the dream, a conversation would occur, but I woke not remembering any of it.

What grew in intensity were the sensations of burning anger, jealousy, judgment, and comparison. I did not know I could feel like this, but here I was, among many others wanting Guruji's attention, suffering these powerful emotions.

The day of my initiation was getting closer. Guruji gave interviews in the chapel and then Darshan on February 16. He was busy the entire day, but towards evening, He finally decided to speak to me. I had several questions I wanted to ask Him. I was standing outside, really beaten, exhausted, and now in pain from the continued activity in my mind.

He came to the chapel door and beckoned me with a stern look. As I entered, I felt trepidation, but as He sat on His chair, He looked at me with so much love, I was disarmed. He smiled broadly and I sat in front of Him. He proceeded to put His right foot on my chest and said I could hold it, which I did.

He looked at me and said, "Oh I see you have questions" and proceeded to answer them without hearing what they were. The first question in my mind was, "Do I know you; do we know each other?" He answered it in this way, "How many times has this foot been on this chest?" Then He said, "I see you want to know what your role is. You are the builder of temples," and immediately my mind carried me to a construction site, with workers, dust, bricks and a crane. He burst out laughing and said, "No, not like this. You will come to understand."

He then stood up and asked if I was in a relationship and I said no. He replied, 'Then it will not be a problem for you to be initiated." He walked ahead of me, opened the door and the smile disappeared. It was back to the firm and distant disciplinarian.

Six days after our conversation, on the morning of my initiation as a Brahmachari, there was no dissipation of the anger and frustration I felt. It was with me throughout the entire ceremony. Derek was my co-initiate as well as two other Mauritian devotees.

The initiation commenced at 9.46 am and by 11.18 am it was over. My days continued much the same, filled with overwhelming emotions as I sat in front of the fish tank, still reading the one thousand names of the Goddess.

The pain in my throat which had started a few days earlier, increased. I had a mild but consistent fever. I still dreamt of Guruji at night, but with no memory of the dream in the morning.

The night of Shivaratri was on Sunday the 26th of February 2006. I was at the height of whatever mental purification was occurring and determined to set myself apart from everything, I watched from the sidelines all the action of the entire night. My mind roared judgment at everyone around Guruji. Then my fury was directed at Him. On several occasions that night, He looked at me from where He was sitting. I gave up trying to stop the stream of pain and watched it as it grew.

Then slowly, Guruji came towards me. Moving through the crowd greeting people, I knew He was headed for me. He stood alongside my chair, looked at me and said, "Are you awake?" My verbal reply was "Yes, I am", but mentally, it was much different. He smiled and returned to where He was sitting.

The day was a buzz of activity. Guruji manifested several lingams in front of us and some alone in His room. Yet I had nothing but judgment and criticism for everything. I felt completely out of control.

Suddenly, I observed a change in Him. He left for almost half an hour, returning after having changed His clothes. My mind had much to say about that too. Then He raised His right hand and in it, He held the Golden Lingam, Hiranyagarbha.

My mind exploded, pouring out evil thoughts like bullets. Guruji placed Hiranyagarbha on the larger lingam for Abhishekam. In my rage, I vowed not to bow to it or Him, yet somehow, minutes later, I found myself on my knees, bowing. We went to bed after 6am and when I woke later that day, I waited for the stormy weather in my mind to continue, but there was nothing.

I was sitting in my usual place alongside the fish tank when Guruji came downstairs. He smiled, I looked at Him in confusion, and said, "I really need to speak with you," and He said, "Yes, I need to speak to you, too." He told me we would speak after breakfast.

I waited at the same spot and caught Him just as He was about to go upstairs to His room. He held my hands and looked at me. I asked, 'What was that?" He knew what I was referring to, and said, "Every Brahmachari must be tested." My immediate reaction was, "How did I do?" He laughed and said, "You felt pain because you did not speak about it."

He then raised His voice, directed His head upwards, and said, "The next time it happens, you should speak about it." I realised He was not just talking to me but to someone else who had also been through something painful. She stopped just out of our sight on the second flight of stairs. I wanted to discuss further, but He made it clear the conversation was over.

I was returning to South Africa a day or so later, so I went shopping, found a photograph of Narasimhadev and brought it back for Him to bless. I attempted to speak about what happened again, but He dismissed it. Now was to come a time of even greater testing that would span about seven years.

CHANGING TRAJECTORIES

Catching up with the changes

When I think back to that first visit to Mauritius, I remember the hurt and confusion following His behaviour towards me. Such actions the mind can conceive. Then there are actions by the Guru that cannot be comprehended, at least not until the mind's limitations have diminished.

One of the first people I contacted upon returning from Mauritius was Yasmin. I was excited to share my experiences with her but also to hear about the progress of a series of spiritual workshops and retreats we started before I left. As Yasmin spoke, I realized the project had fallen apart.

It was a long story that, on the surface, involved issues of money, but as we explored the details, we began to realise there was something else at play. Underlying the drama were the first tremors of seismic spiritual activity that would change our lives forever.

Yasmin and I had been on different paths that converged only a few months earlier. Right from our first meeting, we felt as if we had known each other. We were brought together through unusual circumstances and had a deep spiritual connection. Our natural egoic reaction was to imagine that the reason for our meeting was to combine our spiritual knowledge and share it with others.

Now that the project had collapsed, we were faced with the very strong possibility that it was timeworn and clichéd. We had both been doing the same thing for too long and arrived at a point in our journey where it was time for change but did not pay attention to the signs.

I should have known better. I was a Brahmachari but had not caught up with the fact that I was now on a different trajectory altogether. I would never again be in the world in the same way I was before. Deep in her heart, Yasmin knew that the spiritual life she was living was no longer enough.

New paths open up

We realised a lot later that the project collapsed to reveal a new path, one that we were both now travelling, albeit in different ways. Yasmin, however, had yet to accept that my Guru was hers too.

The Brahmachari work begins

Following the news that we would not be embarking on this line of work; I started speaking to more people about my experiences with Guruji. What I did not realise then, was that through the Brahmachari initiation, Guruji was now working His magic.

I excitedly shared the process of my initiation and everything that occurred to anyone curious. Yasmin listened with an interest seasoned with suspicion. I gave her some of the vibhuti Guruji manifested from His feet, which she accepted with trepidation.

Then she asked to see the photograph of Narasimhadev that Guruji had blessed. Upon seeing it, her first remark was that she knew this 'lion-man' and had seen Him in photos at her teaching sessions. As she held the blessed picture, she asked in bewilderment, "What's happening, what's happening?" She could feel a current of energy travelling through her body that prevented her from letting go of the photograph. The sensation lasted for almost ten minutes before she was finally able to release it.

During one of Guruji's visits that year, I insisted Yasmin see Him. She took Darshan, but to my dismay, she was unable to comprehend who He was and what this meeting held for her.

Many years later, Yasmin found her way to Guruji and is now a committed devotee. I have many stories of people He touched through my association with them. I only realised much later, that after my initiation as a Brahmachari, He placed His flame of Love within me. I found myself unwittingly drawing all His would-be devotees out of their comfort zones, onto a path towards Him.

What I know now is that the Guru's power cannot be comprehended. His calling is deliberate and pre-destined. When it is time, He finds us.

Taken after my Samadhi experience

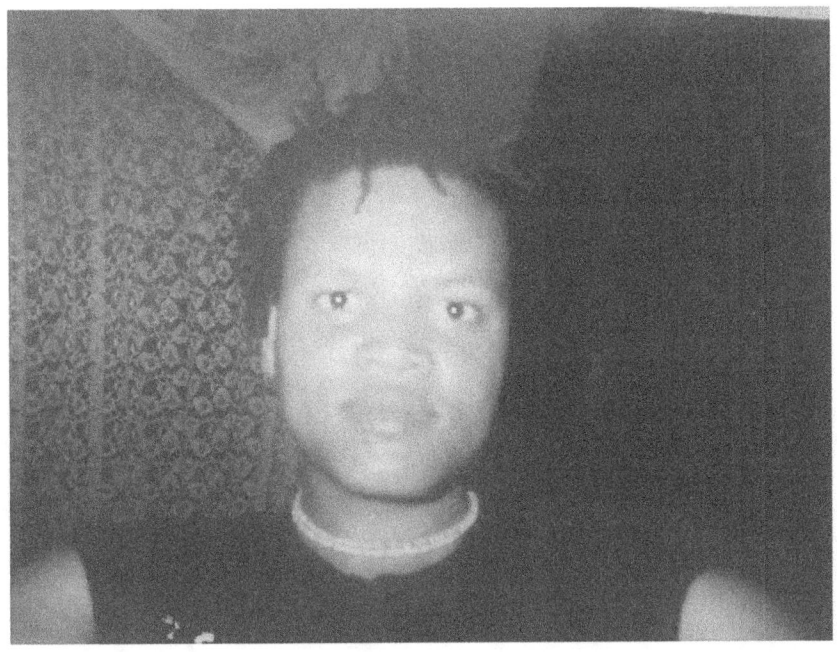

Me, when I was 21 years old, before I met Guruji. This was a selfie before they became cool

Praying to the Divine Mother in Mauritius whom I felt deeply connected to

My first time in Mauritius with Guruji

In Mauritius with Guruji at one of his favourite places

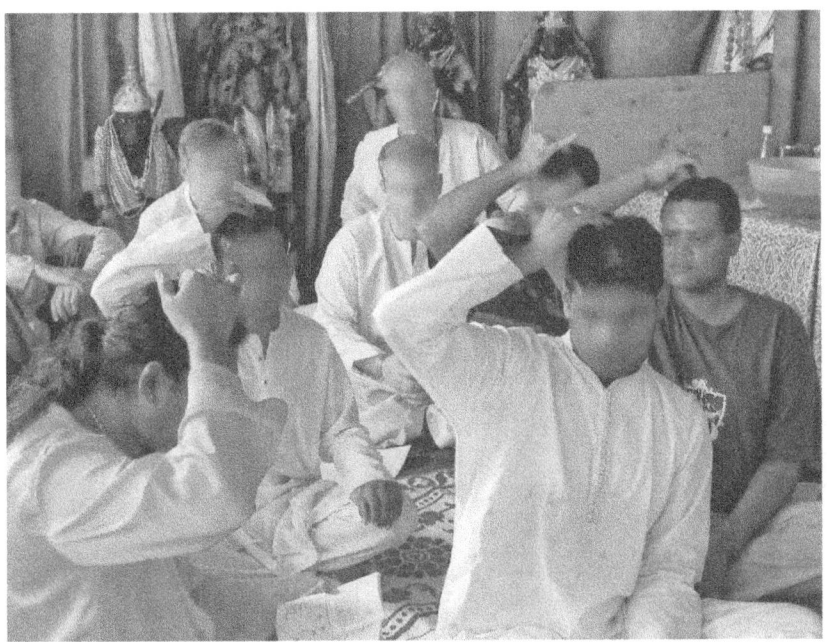

The Brahmachari Initiation ceremony in Mauritius

Shortly after I was initiated as a Brahmachari in 2006. My Brahmachari name was Mangalananda

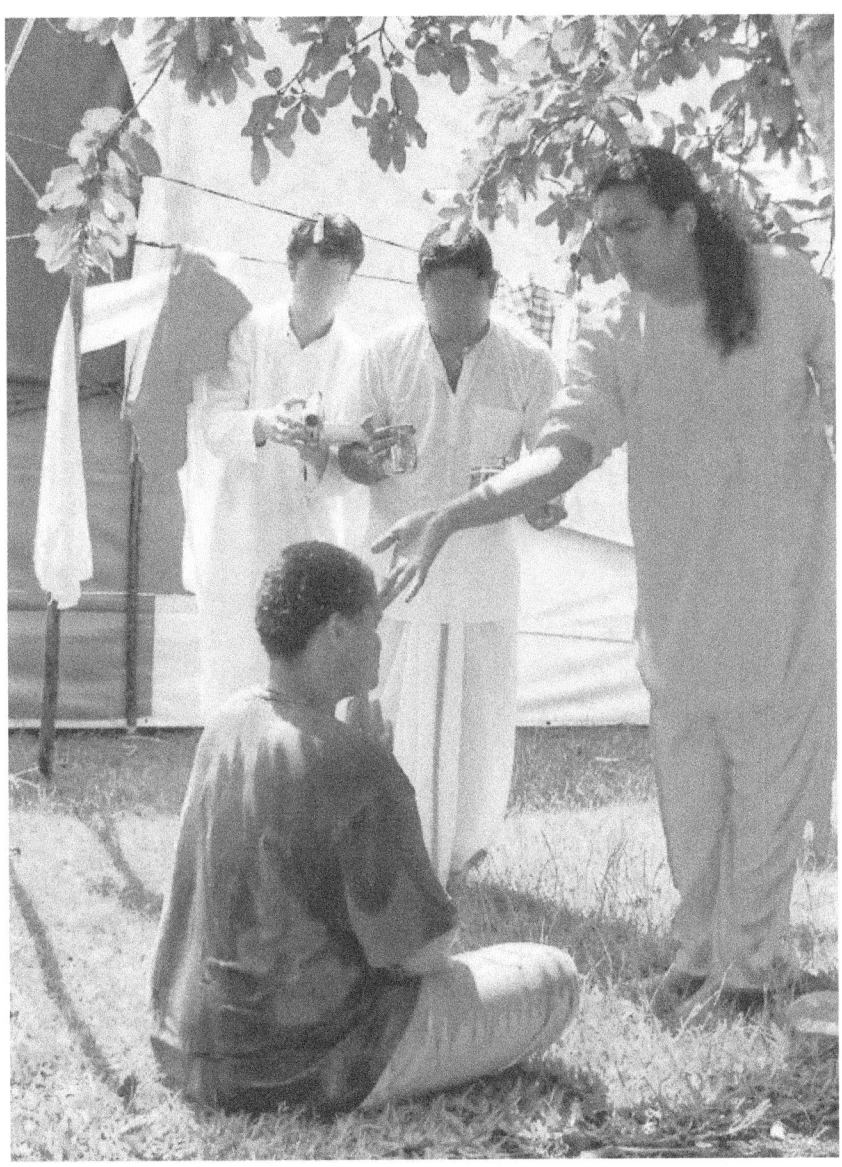

Applying Tilak at the Brahmachari Initiation

The end of the Bramachari ceremony in Mauritius

The first visit of Guruji in South Africa after my Bramachari initiation where we held our first Yagna together

This picture of Guruji was taken in South Africa in 2007 during the Yagna

The Yagna which was spontaneous

In 2008 on a pilgrimage with Guruji

LEARNING TO TRUST THE GURU

Interrogating the Guru

When we find ourselves in uncomfortable circumstances, the first thing we do is question the Guru. We interrogate Him, driven by fear-based suspicious notions. Does He *actually* know what this world is like? Does He *really* know what He's talking about? Are His rules realistic in this day and age? Can He not do things differently, so that we can feel more comfortable? All these questions reveal our ignorance of who He is and our arrogance in thinking we know something He does not.

When Guruji returned to South Africa that year, I found myself doing just that – questioning His decisions. This unfortunate incident came about because He told me that as a Brahmachari, I could no longer physically touch people in my healing practice.

He touches a nerve

I was flabbergasted and thought this was a totally unreasonable request. Naturally, I attempted to bargain with Him. I presented possible conditions under which He ought to allow me to continue, hoping He would consider my reasoning and agree with it.

I told Him I just did not see how this was going to work for me and that there must be some sort of dispensation for Brahmacharis in my situation. I went on and on. I told Him I made my living with my hands and that people expected to be touched. They needed to be touched. What kind of healer did not touch their patients? My healing practice would crash and burn. How would it be possible for me to take care of myself? Where would the money come from? I would be penniless. I would have to live with my mother and accept handouts from her. I would not be able to afford to travel. I would be stuck in Kokstad for the rest of my life, I would be a loser, a waster, a good-for-nothing. My projections were endless and alarming.

Guruji was not at all fazed by my reaction. He was firm and repeated that I could not touch anybody except my mother.

There was no question of me disobeying Him. I presented my argument, but He was undeterred by my protests. I did not understand, but He was my Guru and one of the vows of my initiation was that I place my full trust in Him.

A new way of being

I was plagued with worry as I made my way back to Kokstad. My healing practice was my independence and my freedom. The way I saw it, I would lose both.

There would be no need for me to be in Johannesburg. What would I do now?

Back in Kokstad, the money I saved had run out, and I needed a specific amount to cover some expenses. I made an altar in my room where I was offering service to Guruji. Sitting in front of the altar that morning, I said to Him, 'You have asked me not to touch others, and I surrender to your request. But now I am in need. You are responsible for me.'

About 45 minutes later, I was sitting in the lounge when I heard a knock at the door. It was my friend Nerissa, who lived just a few metres away. She said, "I think you need this," and handed me some money. It was precisely the amount I required.

I asked, "Why are you giving this to me?" She said, "I felt compelled to do it. Out of nowhere, a picture of you came to mind with the thought that you needed this money. I had to act upon it." I told her of my prayer. She looked stunned and left me standing at the door.

Since then, I have always received everything I need. I've come to learn that once we surrender to Him, He takes care of everything.

His request for me to stop touching people had many layers of significance. The enforced discipline triggered the instinctual human fear of survival. As a species, we've disconnected from God to such an extent, that we believe we are alone. We tell ourselves, that we have to do everything in our power to survive.

This is not our natural state but a false idea of ourselves born of disconnection. We belong to God, and it is God who provides everything we need. When we meet our Guru, part of His work involves removing our reliance on ourselves and replacing it with reliance on Him. At first it feels frightening because of our ingrained beliefs, yet we have to trust him totally through the fear.

The idiom 'to take a leap of faith' is exactly what I had to do by giving up my healing practice. Guruji had placed me in a position where I had no one to rely on except Him. For those of us who want to attain Him, for those of us who want freedom, there is a price. He tells us we have to give ourselves up and stop trying to make things happen for ourselves. We ought to look only to Him for sustenance. And once we are in this state, we don't have to ask, because He *knows*.

I knew I had two choices. I could follow my fearful thoughts, break my vows, and carry on working, or I could obey my Guru. I chose Him because life is no longer worth living without Him in it. He was a part of me. It would have felt unnatural to let Him go.

This situation also taught me how ignorant we are when we first come into contact with the Guru. We treat Him as if He is some kind of New Age fad, adaptable to our fanciful and changing needs. We do not realise that He is here to rescue us on terms dictated by God and that *He* holds the answers as to how to transcend this limited world. We have to adapt to His rules and follow

His guidance. We find it difficult to accept that the reason for His rules is beyond anything the mind can conceive. It is only for us to trust His word, and if we cannot do that, then we remain lost in ourselves.

He makes everything possible

In our South African Sangha, I noticed that an initiated devotee was not participating in our weekly fire ceremony. After observing this for about three weeks, I called her aside to ask her the reason why. With some embarrassment, she explained that she was bleeding. I expressed my incredulity, pointing out that she was way past the age of menstrual issues. She indicated that she had indeed been bleeding for more than a year. I asked her if she had sought medical help, and she explained that the doctors she'd seen were unable to ascertain what exactly was causing the bleeding, and so nothing could be done.

I asked her if she had thought to go inward and ask Guruji for assistance. She seemed surprised by this question and said she decided it was not possible because the 'men of science' had said so. I explained that Guruji does not heal everyone on request, because there are times when our illnesses present spiritual gifts of transformation. There are other times, however, when He will intervene. It is a matter of trust, and our ability to hand over the issue to Him.

With that in mind, I told her to go inward and lay everything at Guruji's feet and then to see a specialist gynaecologist.

Since it usually takes several months to see a specialist, we were both shocked when she received an appointment with the gynaecologist only two days after she visited the GP.

During her examination by the gynaecologist, she ardently prayed to Guruji, thanking Him for His presence. Amusingly, she also apologised to Guruji for the situation in which she found herself, as she was naked, with her legs up in stirrups at the time! I assured her that this would have no bearing on Guruji.

As she continued her inner dialogue with Guruji, the doctor who was examining her asked her if she was praying. She replied that she was indeed talking to her Guru whom she felt was present in the room.

The doctor established the problem was a non-invasive tumour in her cervix that would require surgical removal.

Arriving at the surgery the next day, she noticed that the entire office had been transformed into a miniature surgical unit. The doctor and her secretary, who was to act as an assistant in the surgery, were now ready to perform the procedure. The doctor also explained to her that she would not be administering an anaesthetic and asked if that would be acceptable.

She looked at the situation and all the steps that had brought her there and she could see only Guruji's kindness and compassion. She replied, "Yes, thank you, I am okay with that". She mentally put herself and whatever was happening, and whatever the result would be, at Guruji's feet.

The procedure was over in less than half an hour. When the time came to pay for the procedure, she discovered the doctor's assistant had already prepared the receipt. The devotee's heart started to beat heavily as there was no way she could afford such a costly procedure. Taking a pen from the desk, the doctor scratched out that large figure, and replaced it with an amount she had in her purse! She wept in gratitude.

She asked me to please convey her message of eternal thankfulness to Guruji for His role in her life. The biopsy results came back a few weeks later as negative.

He knows what's right

I recall a time when Guruji received a message from a devotee He had known for more than 20 years. She simply declared to Him, 'I am afraid.' She was facing the last moments of her life, and she knew that He could change the entire circumstance simply by His will. She said to Him, 'I know you can remove this from me.'

Since this was so intimate a moment, I prepared to leave the space, but He asked me to stay and listen to their conversation. He said to her, 'No, you should never be afraid. What is coming now – I will be with you.' I could hear the sadness in her voice as she struggled with the reality that Guruji was telling her that it was time for her to move on.

What struck me the most was the look in His eyes. Everything about Him became about care and acceptance. I saw Him holding her through this transition which would take several days, during which He spoke to her at the end of every day. Regardless of what He was doing, He offered her His presence every day at the end of her life.

Letting go

This is what Guruji means when He says we must let go of our self-reliance and replace it with reliance on Him. We have to trust that He knows what is right for us, and that He knows where we need to be at any point in our existence. Our limited mind places boundaries on reality; it has certain expectations and does not accept anything that goes against those expectations. It also insists that certain things are not possible. Yet, in leaving everything to Him, in laying our lives at His feet, we always find ourselves in the right place at the right time, and in trusting Him, everything becomes possible.

MY FIRST VISIT TO INDIA

The significance of travel

Guruji often spoke of the primary reason people travel. He called it 'self-entertainment'. He said we travel to satisfy our senses, to see, hear and taste something different. With such narrow expectations, we do not expand our outlook on life, we do not grow.

What we don't realise is that travel is an inner journey that transforms us. The more we open ourselves to different experiences, the more the mind expands.

In the beginning, before I met Guruji, my reasons for travel were centred on learning and acquiring skills. Later, they became about sharing skills. After spending time with Guruji and being affected by His love, and the way He is in the world, my travels became about sharing Him with others. This was a gradual process during which the way I saw the world and everyone in it, altered.

India

The first time I travelled to India was after I watched a series of pilgrimages on DVD, featuring several Jyotirlinga (material manifestations of Shiva), holy cities and towns. I was completely mesmerised and watched the DVDs again and again, creating a strong intent to visit as many of those places as possible. I would take mental snapshots of each place knowing that someday I would visit each one. I looked at the images and learnt the names and locations of places where I could stay nearby.

Having no idea how to plan a tour to a foreign country, I did the best I could on my own. There were no direct flights to Delhi from South Africa.

I endured the procedure of obtaining a visa, and flight tickets and allocating a budget for land transport. I did not anticipate any pitfalls, although there were many.

I arrived in Mumbai at about 4am. I did not expect the sheer volume of human beings in hurried activity this early in the morning. The air was humid and permeated by a peculiar smell. It felt much older than any other city I had ever been to.

I hailed a taxi and asked to be taken to the main train station so I could book my tickets to Delhi and had to wait along with hundreds of others at the station, many sleeping on the floor while they waited. Everything was so foreign to me including seeing a cow with its head in a shack while the inhabitants slept outside because the night was so warm.

My mind was gathering and processing information at an unrecognizable speed. There were street dogs everywhere. Hundreds of them. The noise from people and traffic, the intensity of activity, and the rich odours of human life left me in stupefied awe.

When the ticketing counter eventually opened around 7am, there was a system of queuing I had not experienced before. Not knowing a word of Hindi did not help. Eventually, somebody pointed to a counter for tourists and with some difficulty, I managed to book a ticket to Delhi for later that afternoon on the Rajdhani Express. This was my first train ride since I was seven or eight years old.

With hours to go before departure, I asked a taxi driver to take me to the nearest and cheapest hotel where I managed to grab some respite from the busy external environment and enjoyed some much-needed sleep.

Travelling to Delhi from Mumbai was by far the longest train trip I had ever made. I became aware of the sheer size of India and how the smell of cities changed as we travelled ever north. Travelling through the desert in Rajasthan and Gujarat, I saw massive rivers and beautiful natural scenery.

Before travelling to India, people told me about the poverty and squalor I would encounter. I only saw this in the big cities. Travelling through the different regions, I gained a new sense of gratitude for the life I had, and for the opportunity I had to visit such a beautiful country.

The hours passed and we arrived in Delhi. Disembarking from the train, my senses were beset by more distinct smells. After lugging my bag up and down several flights of stairs, I realised that everybody was stopping to stare at me because there was no one else around who shared my ethnic background. I found their intense curiosity quite disconcerting.

Haridwar

I had no idea how or where to board the train to Haridwar. I saw several taxis and made the fatal mistake every new traveller makes. I boarded a car with no air-conditioning and only then asked the price for a five-hour trip to Haridwar. To be fair, I was tired of travelling and just really wanted to get to my destination. After some blind 'negotiation' and agreement on a somewhat dubious price for the service, we headed out.

The countryside changed continuously as we made our way through lush thick forests, mountainous rocky terrain, and farmland. There were cows everywhere. Many were standing in groups in the middle of roads riddled with potholes. The driver explained that the heavy downpours of the rainy season were responsible for the disappearance of the roads in many areas.

Finally, we arrived on the outskirts of Haridwar when the driver made an illegal turn through a red traffic light, right in front of several police officers who were ready to arrest him. I discover he is not a local driver, and he gets pulled over by the police. It is easy for the police officers to extract a bribe from him and he, of course, turns to me to pay the bribe.

The Ganges River was as beautiful as it looked in all the documentaries I had watched. The river was wide, the water pristinely clean and it flowed swiftly into the distance. There was a slight chill in the air due to the proximity of the large body of water. I inhaled a different smell and felt the sacred energy of the city of Haridwar move within me. This was to become one of my favourite places to visit.

Suddenly the driver stopped and said he was unable to take me any further. I protested, reminding him that he was paid to take me to the hotel. He pretended not to understand, and I simply gave up. I got out of his car right there next to the Ganges. Fortunately, there was a cycle rickshaw willing to take me to the Ashok Hotel.

I arrived! The excitement I felt was indescribable. I was elated. At the age of twenty-six I had successfully travelled on my own to India – one of the holiest places in the world. I could hardly wait to explore it.

Blessings from Haridwar

I rested in my hotel for a while, then went for my first walk, feeling the heartbeat of Haridwar and allowing the humidity to embrace me. The aromas in the evening air drew me to a market with quaint and interesting places to eat.

I then headed to Hari ki Pauri, one of the most sacred bathing ghats in India which looked exactly as I remembered it in the documentary I watched. I approached the water and immediately submerged my feet and hands. At first, it felt icy cold against the sticky heat of the evening. The aroma of incense, flickering of little lamps, sounds of bells, and hooting of cars and motorcycles, became the first imprint of Haridwar in my mind and heart. I felt content and planned to spend several days here before I could determine how I would travel to other places that held my interest. For now, I was basking in the deep undercurrent of peace and allowing the ancient spiritual forces to bathe me. My gratitude to God for my Guru, and for reconciling with something unnameable and forgotten. Merged with the energy of Haridwar, I felt reborn.

In the next few days, I watched thousands of people descend on the Ganges, honouring her sacred waters, taking refuge and asking for blessings over their families.

Lessons from Haridwar

Moving around Haridwar, I became acutely aware that all we have is what we come into this life with. Never have I seen such acceptance of circumstance. People with next to nothing, accede to what is, instead of questioning what should be and live in a state of Grace, relying on the Gods to make their wishes a reality. It is a completely different mindset from the one that governs the lives of the vast majority of people in India and the outside world.

I realise how we, influenced by Western standards, measure success based on our material acquisitions. Matters of the soul and our relationship with God are a distant second. Even those who call themselves religious are on the outside looking in, never really embracing the truth of what God is. I realized it is us who decide who God is, His role and position in our lives. We expect handouts from God – for Him to provide according to our material desires. We pray for things; not for Him. When He does not deliver, we reject Him. Because of this total misunderstanding of who God is, we are lost to who we are, why we are here, and how we can find ourselves again.

In Haridwar, the people have gained something. They have reached a place where they know their lives are governed by God and accept this – whether they like their conditions of living or not. They live in poverty and experience hardship, yet understand that this is their path. They might not have the full picture of who God is, or what the relationship demands, but they are closer to the truth than most of us. While we endlessly try to attain peace through material gain and put God on the backburner, they have come to a place of acceptance of His will. They have more than we have. But I only see that now.

Pilgrimage

I began thinking about the next phase of my journey and joyfully anticipated fulfilling yet another spiritual aspiration – the Char Dham pilgrimage.

'Char' means 'four', and 'Dham' means 'holy place'. This pilgrimage navigates the holy sites of Gangotri, Yamunotri, Kedarnath and Badrinath, all tucked away in the colossal heights of the Himalayas. These four Hindu Temples are situated at the source of four holy rivers: the Ganges River at Gangotri Temple, the Yamuna River at Yamunotri, the Mandakini River at Kedarnath Temple, and the Alaknanda River at Badrinath Temple.

Many believe that a pilgrimage to these places is a sacred journey that all Hindus must take at least once in their lifetime. To say how excited I was, is an understatement since I viewed these pilgrimages on DVD more often than I can remember.

Haridwar is an official departing point for Char Dham, and a hive of activity for pilgrimage tourism. I was directed by hotel staff to a company called Garwal Mandal Vikas Nigum, a government-run association that facilitates transportation, accommodation and food for people who wish to complete the Char Dham pilgrimage.

The assistant travel officer was taken aback when I informed him I would be alone on the pilgrimage, as this is traditionally experienced with family. Nevertheless, he calculated the costs and told me what I had to do to get to where I had to go. I was hopping with excitement and felt like a child, imagining all the things I would see for the very first time.

Taken by the spirit of holy pilgrimage, I decided to eat nothing but mangoes for the duration. It would benefit me spiritually and save me a bit of money.

I departed early the next morning. That evening at dinner, I saw everybody who would be with me the following week as we traversed the sacred Himalayan Mountains. The bus was a small thirty-two-seater and as the travel officer in Haridwar had informed me, it was populated by families consisting of four or five people. There were parents, grandparents and children, ranging in age from five to seventy years old. Seeing how important this journey was for them, offered me yet another insight into a uniquely different way of being in the world.

I sat towards the back of the bus and observed the passengers. My fellow Hindu pilgrims were from vastly different backgrounds, and had different socio-economic standings, yet all believed in the importance of the Char Dham pilgrimage. Something in me stirred; I was among people whose lives were rooted in a Divinity I was searching for. This growing realization in me that we are all born in places that mirror our inner relationship with God began to dominate my thinking. I was born into a world that is distanced from God. Where I am from, God is an idea we shape around our belief systems. He does not inform our way of thinking, or our behaviour. Instead, we tend to make God fit our expectations and practices.

Here, Hindus defer to God, meaning their cultural beliefs and behaviours are generally guided by God. Nobody here is perfect, and when it matters most, not everyone stays true to their Hindu beliefs. But God is the presence they bask in. This realisation had a massive impact on me.

The journey to Gangotri

I shared the excitement as we began our journey into the mountains at around 6.30 am. The tour guide explained that the journey would end at a high altitude, and then announced the stop-off en route. He informed us that these frequent stops were measures taken for our bodies to adjust to the increasing altitude and would help to mitigate or even prevent the symptoms of altitude sickness which were most commonly felt by symptoms such as nausea and headache.

It was the tail-end of the rainy season. As the roads snaked and climbed steeply into the embrace of the Himalayan Mountains, my eyes searched the landscape for different trees and unusual flowers. My love of nature was heightened by the beauty of this landscape.

The first stop of the day was Joshimath. My mango fast had not begun yet, so I ordered some chickpeas. It turned out to be the worst decision I could have made. They were undercooked, flavourless and contributed to an uncomfortable bout of indigestion. We stayed overnight in Joshimath, and the next day journeyed towards Gangotri, the source of the holy Ganges.

The Gangotri trail

We reached Gomukh, the starting point of the hiking trail that leads to the Gangotri Temple, seventeen kilometres above. I needed to hire a horse, since the path was slippery. I could think of nothing more inconvenient than falling in the mud.

The progress was slow, and I was amazed at the ease with which the guide leading the horse navigated the narrow path. I absorbed as much as I could, allowing the precious sights to be imprinted in my memory. I did not want to forget even a second of this experience. Growing in moss on the rockface were the tiniest little orchids and plants I had ever seen.

The sheer volume of people pushing themselves up this inhospitable gradient fascinated me. I kept asking myself how so many people could share such a deep spiritual conviction. Discovering such a place in the world where God is central to life, aspiration is Divine in nature, and pilgrimage is travel where profound transformation is assumed.

Gangotri Temple

We approach the temple complex of Gangotri, dedicated to Goddess Ganga. According to history, King Bhagirath worshipped Lord Shiva at a sacred stone situated near where the Temple now stands. This stone was later to be called the Bhagirathi Shila. It is said that Lord Shiva was so happy with King Bhagirath, that He summoned the Goddess Ganga, who at that time was a celestial river. He took Her into His dreadlocks and released Her onto the spot where King Bhagirath meditated. The Goddess was so pleased with King Bhagirath that She washed away the sins of his ancestors with Her holy waters. She also became his spiritual daughter, as he was responsible for Her appearance on Earth. The Ganges river is also called by the name of Bhagirathi, meaning 'Bhagiratha's daughter'.

The water was icy cold and the temple resplendently beautiful. Throngs of people were here to pay their respects to the Goddess. Some of them sat in the courtyard of the temple, reciting prayers, and asking favours of the Goddess. Others performed Yagna for their ancestors on the banks of the Bhagirathi, in the belief that actions like these would free their ancestors from the cycle of rebirth. According to history, the Pandavas had performed those same ancestral rituals to free the spirits of their family members who died in the Kurukshetra war.

Nearby is a series of hot springs. The journey is not over until we all participate in the traditional bath to cleanse ourselves of our sins. Almost immediately after, we began the journey back down the mountain.

The Journey to Yamunotri

Our next destination was Yamunotri, the temple close to the glacial source of the Yamuna River. We cross several valleys as our driver navigates a road so narrow, it cannot accommodate two-way traffic. The sounds of car hooters pervade the crisp mountain air, cautioning us of their presence. No one wants to hurtle hundreds of feet down the mountainside. Twice in our journey to Yamunotri, we crossed through a waterfall; it was exhilarating and terrifying at the same time. The reality of the danger was made evident by numerous abandoned cars on the cliff face. Some were swept away by landslides, others were crushed by huge rocks that descended from the heights above the road. I wondered how many pilgrims were aware of the dangers before they left home.

As I reminisce on the hazards of this trip, I remember; the outer journey of pilgrimage is an inner journey to find God. To find God within, is a fearful journey for the mind, because a recognition of the Divine Self is always accompanied by massive change. Peering from the bus window into the murky depths of canyons which swallowed the lives of so many, I prayed silently for us to make it to our next destination.

On route, we encountered a car stuck in a stream, blocking the way for anyone to move in either direction on the narrow road. As everyone moved to offer aid to the driver, more cars arrived from both directions. Nobody appeared to be flustered. No one was in a rush. Everyone just accepted the situation and did their part to help.

Arriving in the hamlet of Yamunotri much later than planned, the curiosity of my fellow pilgrims got the better of them. They began to ask me questions. They wanted to know why I was alone, why I was on this pilgrimage and *who* I was.

I started to share my story and spoke at length about Guruji. I found myself answering questions I would not ordinarily have known the answer to. I was surprised by this flow of intuitive knowledge, but in later years became accustomed to it. When we let go of ourselves for just a moment, Guruji speaks through us, and just in bringing Him to mind with all our love, He is fully present in that moment. This discourse heightened their interest and later that night, I received knocks on my hotel room door with further requests for spiritual dialogue.

My fellow pilgrims voiced extreme concern about my diet of mangoes. Each one tried to ascertain the reason and expressed amazement when I told them that since we were visiting temples, I preferred to keep it simple so as to focus better. They were really impressed by my discipline yet still would not stop offering all kinds of snacks. They tried to feed me and were disturbed by my rejection of dried fruit and spiced roti.

The Yamunotri Temple

We headed out on the six-kilometre trek to Yamunotri the next morning. Approaching the Temple, we passed brightly coloured prasad shops, blaring music, burning incense and people trying to get us to buy their trays of offerings from shops selling all manner of religious paraphernalia.

Yamunotri is the origin of the river Yamuna. Containing the Goddess Yamuna in black marble majestic and awe-inspiring. As I bask in the holy energy, I allow my mind to be overwhelmed by the Divine within me. I know now that as we come across places permeated with the energy of saints and Gods, we encounter the Divine reality of who we are. There are no words; there is only spiritual recognition the mind expresses as absolute awe.

Among the hot springs at Yamunotri is a well that contains boiling water. People put potatoes and rice tied in special cloth and offer this food cooked at the shrine of the Goddess Yamuna to be eaten as prasad.

The hot springs there were a joy to bathe in, but we could not remain immersed, as I learned from experience that the sulphur and minerals the water contains irritate the skin.

The mountain temples are beautiful against the imposing backdrop of the Himalayan mountains. Walking back from Yamunotri, it started to rain. In our haste to escape the downpour, my fellow pilgrims and I rushed past a small hut from which a sadhu shouted, "Hey South Africa!"

Being wet, and anxious to return to my room, I did not stop to answer his call. My mind, however, was overtaken by the mystery of people like this. How did this stranger know me? We were all foreign to these parts. None of us had seen him before. Later, on subsequent pilgrimages, I learnt that saddhus like him walk between worlds. They have transcended in a way that we can never truly understand, yet they continue to wander for the greater welfare of others.

During this extraordinary trip, my evenings included listening to Guruji singing on my portable tape player, while recalling the smells and sounds of the day. I wondered about the lives of the people who lived in the villages close to the places of pilgrimage. I wished we could stay longer in each location.

Kedernath

There were two more places to see on this Char Dham pilgrimage; Badrinath and Kedarnath.

Kedarnath is one of the most important of the twelve Jyotirlinga. The Jyotirlinga Temples are places where Lord Shiva manifested as columns of light, and within the Temples are lingams which are devotional representations of Him.

Unfortunately, it was an ancient temple I would not get to see, as it was clear that if I spent the money on the tour, I would not have any for the remainder of the pilgrimage. I spent the day walking around the village, learning the history of Kedarnath and resting in my room.

Badrinath

Despite all the preventative measures I had taken, I still felt symptoms of altitude sickness, but the anticipation of this visit overpowered it. After a long and arduous journey to Badrinath, I looked forward to seeing Lord

Vishnu, who manifested as the black granite deity of Lord Badrinath. Everything I read about other people's experiences swam through my mind.

Seeing the temple for the first time, it was an explosion of colours against the backdrop of a huge and imposing mountain. It remains one of the most popular temples to visit, and for me was the easiest temple to reach. I wondered who lived there and why they would choose to live there.

With the sun setting in the background, we reached Lord Badrinath, greeted by the distinct fragrance of worship. Again, I was awestruck by the antiquity of the temple and the thought of thousands of people gathering here every year to render worship and ask for the fulfilment of wishes. I felt deeply privileged to be partaking in rituals older than I could imagine. I could not have known at this time how this pilgrimage was to be an integral part of a Divine plan for my life, and that future pilgrimages with Guruji would further enrich my spiritual life.

We stayed overnight in Badrinath. The plan was to head to Uttarkashi the next day and, after lunch, move to Rishikesh. However, things did not go to plan.

Uttarkashi

When we reached Uttarkashi, we received the news that we could not journey on to Rishikesh because a mudslide had completely covered the road. We were stuck in Uttarkashi and the inclement weather made it uncomfortable to venture outside.

At this point, I had very little money left to do what I wanted to do in India. My initial plan was to spend time in the Dayanada Ashram in Rishikesh. While laid up in Uttarkashi, I used the time to calculate how I could maximise my budget. At this time, I did not have a bank account so I could not even ask for money to be transferred. It seemed like a complete impossibility, yet I held out hope for some kind of miracle.

After three days of waiting, everyone became increasingly impatient. The driver had been told of an alternate route through a deserted town. While it would take longer, everyone felt it would be better than just waiting.

After another gruelling journey through perilous terrain, the lights of Rishikesh in the distance were a huge comfort.

Rishikesh

In Rishikesh, one of the people at the travel offices helped me to plan yet another pilgrimage. He was very kind and calculated the costs for the entire itinerary and offered his services to arrange everything whenever I wanted. I told him I wanted to go to the Dayananda Ashram and since it was just a few houses away from where he lived, he offered to drop me there when he was done with work. I felt relieved and grateful for His kind offer.

The Dayananda Ashram

Later that afternoon, my big grey bag and I arrived at the Dayananda Ashram, a place that would become my 'home away from home' whenever I returned to Rishikesh. Situated on the banks of the Ganga, the Ashram was founded during the 1960s by Swami Dayananda Saraswati, a highly revered teacher of Vedanta and Sanskrit. All the teachings are rooted in the Divine knowledge acquired through the direct experience of the ancient Rishis of India. My breathing stopped as I stood outside. I had arrived.

The receptionists at the Ashram explained the system and asked about the duration of my stay. They seemed unfazed when I responded with an estimate of three weeks. I was still trying to work out how I would pay for these three weeks because by now, my meagre cash reserves had dried up.

A whole new education

I decided to take things one day at a time and enjoy what I could in the moment. The Dayananda Ashram hosts a three-year resident's course, covering a traditional Vedic education for anyone who wishes to study Vedanta. I was allowed to attend all of the classes and through this, I learned how a traditional Vedic education was structured. At that time, the students were in their second year and came from all over the world including India.

I found the Vedic approach to spirituality interesting. The dedication, determination and hard work of the young students was admirable and refreshing.

I was also of great interest to them, and we often spent long hours talking. I made friends with one of the Bramacharis who was in the process of committing his entire life to living in the Ashram and serving his Guru's mission. He enthralled me with stories of the holy men he met in Rishikesh. It was here that the relationship between Guru and disciple became very clear to me. I saw the way the students treated their teacher and I marvelled at the reverence they had for the founder of their Ashram.

This whole experience focused my mind on Guruji. I realised that Guruji was not just a normal person, but something more – far more. I felt it at a deep level, but I had not fully processed what I sensed. Only now, here in this place where extraordinary ways of living in the world exist, could I begin to understand. From the recitation of the Bhagavad Gita that was part of the morning class, I saw many similar qualities between Guruji and Krishna.

Only a miracle

One morning in the Temple, as my time to leave India was fast approaching, I requested Divine assistance for my financial predicament. I longed to complete this trip in the way I had planned. My only hope now lay in handing it over to God. As I walked out of the temple, I walked into the person who facilitated my conversion to Hinduism in Pietermaritzburg some years before. We were both astonished to see each other in a location so far from our first meeting. I soon learnt that he was a graduate of the Dayananda three-year Vedanta programme.

In the course of our conversation, I told him about my money situation, and his immediate response was, "Let me help, how much do you need?"

When I told him I would repay him when he came back to South Africa, he just laughed. We did not end up spending time together, as he had a busy itinerary, but I now felt more relaxed and was able to see more of Rishikesh and its surroundings. I went back to the Temple and offered prayers of thanks for what I believe was a miracle.

Happy, and feeling safe in the love of God, I settled my bill and booked a taxi to Delhi.

A new resolve

It is fair to say that I was not the same after I returned from India. The change in me was obvious in the way I related to people. I felt a determination to live differently, to live for a different purpose. I had seen so many people all over India committed to the same purpose that I was now focused on – serving God.

I resolved not to try to control the events of my life, not to push, to force or to wish for anything. I learnt from my travels that everything will happen in its time and that we are always given what we need.

TRIALS BY FIRE

A trip with Guruji

My relationship with Guruji solidified in different ways after I undertook the Brahmachari initiation. The several trips we made became a way for me to further understand myself. A key time of learning was a six-week pilgrimage to India with Guruji in 2008.

As we landed in Mumbai, we arrived at the Hare Krishna centre on Juhu beach. The rules were explained, which included the dress code for women and men, and we were also given guidelines to follow when venturing into the different Ashrams we were to visit.

Since many of us had only known Guruji for a very short time, this was an opportunity to be in close proximity with Him. I was really excited about this. At this point, Guruji and I were not friends. He was present, but there was a distinct distance between us.

Laddu Gopal

One day, we came upon Guruji in an animated state. He excitedly expressed how He found a deity that had been looking for Him. He described a dream He had about Laddu Gopal – the child form of Lord Krishna – and explained how the deity asked to be found by Him.

In the dream, Laddu Gopal gave several hints to Guruji as to where He was to be found, and so during His search, Guruji found Himself knocking on the door of a stranger asking, "Do you have some old statues of deities?" The person replied, "I don't. But I have many belongings of my father and among them there are deities."

Guruji looked through them and found different representations of Laddu Gopal, but none of them were the deity that was seeking Him.

He went back to the balcony of the place where He was staying, and as He sat there looking out onto the road in front of the building, He noticed a pile of rubbish. In that pile, He could discern what looked like a little black feather. Assuming it was the feather from Lord Krishna's headwear, He ran downstairs, crossed the road, and began rummaging through the rubbish. There under all of it was Laddu Gopal.

Lessons from Laddu Gopal

Guruji teaches us in so many ways. Through this episode, He reminded us that God wants to be found, and that it is *us* who have lost Him. In other words, He has not abandoned us. And how have we lost Him? By building a life based on ideas and concepts far removed from the principles of Love that are our true nature.

These ideas and principles we live by represent the rubbish we bury Him under, and there is so much of it that we can no longer see or feel Him. Yet, regardless of this, He is always trying to make Himself heard, always trying to remind us of our true nature.

Even when we do begin to hear Him, and we set out to discover what this inner calling means, we often find ourselves with different teachers, different gurus who might resemble realized Masters but are not quite the real deal yet.

I experienced many such analogies in the days we travelled from place to place. Many of the sites we visited with Guruji were the Ashrams of other gurus. As we travelled, Guruji asked us to keep a record of our thoughts; and to make notes on how the Ashrams affected us, as well as our feelings about the gurus and devotees who lived in them. This was a pilgrimage, and He wanted us to pay attention to everything.

Dark foreboding

Arriving in Madurai we were received in a small house where we had a pleasant meal with our hosts.

The next day was very painful. Guruji wanted to speak to His group of devotee pilgrims, so we gathered in one of the private rooms. It was stiflingly hot. He sat in a chair while we sat around Him. What He said was shocking.

He explained that He had visited Mahavatar Babaji and went about describing in detail His beauty, and the Divine energy He emanated. But what Babaji said to Guruji when first meeting Him was, "Your Brahmacharis are disobedient."

Guruji then proceeded to ask us how we think it felt for Him to hear that. I remember everybody's head hanging in shame. Devotees were searching their memory to recall incidents of disobedience. The atmosphere was heavy with uncertainty and disappointment.

Next, Guruji said that He knew that a challenging time was approaching and that by the same time next year, half of us would have left Him. The incident that would occur would challenge everything we believed about ourselves, Him and the intricate relationship between Guru and disciple.

I burst into tears thinking of the betrayal and pain He knew was about to occur, and I felt bereft that we would be responsible. My distress increased as I tried to imagine what role I would play.

People in the room eventually rose up in indignant protest, affirming their loyalty, love, and commitment to Guruji. He sat quietly through this outburst, knowing the truth of what was in our hearts, and what would happen in the near future. All I could do was cry at the possibility of losing the person who had just found me.

Testing times in Bangalore

This changed the mood for the rest of the trip. Everyone was on alert. It did not change Him though. He was still holding each of us in His Love as we made the long journey from Madurai to Bangalore by bus.

We visited several major Ashrams on the way, and everyone was writing what they felt. At different points, Guruji would ask to read what we had written. Occasionally He offered a response.

When we finally reached Bangalore, Guruji spent an entire day searching for the deities that would eventually be housed in the temple in Germany. Meanwhile, most of us were laid up because we had fallen sick from eating or drinking something in Madurai.

On one of the days, we planned to spend the evening with Guruji, eating and hopefully, listening to Satsang. He was in a very good mood and shared what He found while shopping for deities. Afterwards, He called on one of the devotees from England and asked her some questions about what she had written about one of our visits to a particular Ashram. In questioning her, He insinuated that she had become upset after her fellow pilgrims had made some negative judgments about the Ashram guru, and a saint she once followed. Guruji was concerned that she had become affronted by their judgment, and in berating their behaviour in her journal, she was blind to the fact that she too was being judgmental about her fellow pilgrims. He needed her to acknowledge the hypocrisy.

She adamantly denied she had written anything of the sort. He asked, "Are you sure?" When she said "Yes", He then pulled out a piece of paper from His pocket and read what she had written. In reading it aloud so she could realize the judgment, He was offering her the opportunity to let go and move on. Instead, she walked away and refused to return even when He called her. She left that day and never returned. Her pride and indignation were greater than her love for Him.

I felt so disturbed by this that when I reached my room, I had a bout of vomiting which went on and on for an inordinate amount of time.

I thought to myself and prayed that I may never make the mistake of placing my feelings above any lesson Guruji gives to me. Little did I know that He would give me a demonstration of this very soon.

Pride

Guruji was invited to the International Yoga Festival in Rishikesh. From Bangalore we flew to Delhi, and from Delhi we travelled by bus to Rishikesh. The International Yoga Festival was hosted by Parmath Niketam, the largest Ashram in Rishikesh. Yoga traditions and schools from all over the world were represented at this event.

On arrival, we were designated rooms and Guruji looked at me and said I should share the apartment offered to Him as there was sufficient room. It had two bedrooms and a very large living space. There was a bed just outside Guruji's bedroom and it was here that He told me I could sleep. We attended several of the classes, listened to some lectures and Guruji gave a demonstration of dancing and singing the Divine Name, which attracted the attention of many of the festival goers. It certainly was not conventional yoga. He explained the concept of love, dancing and singing the name of God.

We watched, participated, and enjoyed. The next day Guruji said to me, "I would like to take a dip in the Ganges, will you please come with me?" Of course, I felt elated to be with Him, and we walked to the Ganges.

The water was extremely cold, and so I stood on the shore while Guruji took His dip. As soon as He surfaced from the river, we began walking back to the apartment. As we approached, He asked, "Can I tell you something?" I nodded, and He declared, "I see pride in you."

My stomach did somersaults. My mind, in a split second of absolute frenzy, tried to find moments on this trip where I could have demonstrated pride. Disappointment and despair turned to rage as I stood there looking at Him. Then I began judging Him, wondering what His motives were, and why He would say such a thing. We walked back to the room in silence; I was lost for words.

Once I calmed down, I resolved to find out if what He said about me was true. Could He be right? As I sat on the bed of my room, my mind embarked on an exhaustive mental search. I reached as far back as the beginning of the tour and mentally travelled step by step through the different legs of the journey. I completely missed the point that it was not necessarily during these recent moments where I exhibited pride. I know now that He was talking about my prideful mindset, my ideas, attitudes, and behaviours at that time. These were not obvious to me, so He took it upon Himself to point it out. Pride is one of the biggest hurdles to God-realization, and it manifests in many insidious ways. But I was yet to understand all of this. All I felt was a huge internal struggle to comprehend what Guruji was trying to teach me.

Suddenly He appeared at my door, His eyes filled with compassion. Sitting next to me, He said, "You don't have to worry, I will take care of it."

My response was childish and petulant: "It's ok, just leave me alone." The kindness in His eyes turned to sadness. I did not have it in me to react in any other way, such was my elusive pride. He did as I asked and left the room.

Since I was so busy mulling over all of this, there was no real interaction with Him for the remainder of the pilgrimage.

Guruji's authority

Arriving in Kankhal, Haridwar, we visited the Samadhi of Anandamayi Ma, who was recognised as one of the great Hindu saints of the 20th Century. Guruji's authority as a realised Master first became evident here.

We walked around the compound. At the back of the Samadhi Mandir was a small house where Anandamayi Ma had lived. Since it was lunchtime, everything was locked, so we peered through the window to get a glimpse into Ma's old life. We could see a bed sheet stained with little droplets of oil. This had been the sheet that covered the bed when Ma received massages; the drops of oil staining the sheet were from the massages.

We moved to her place of Samadhi, and I watched as Guruji prayed at her shrine. His manner of prayer suggested He was asking something of her. Once we were done, He asked everyone to return to the bus. He wanted us to wait whilst He did what He always does at the place of a saint – ask for a relic. To the rest of us pilgrims, it seemed impossible because there was no one of authority that could help with the request. It was just after lunchtime and the residents of the Ashram were taking a nap.

We watched from the bus as He stood still in the middle of the road. Just ahead, a devotee of Anandamayi Ma was walking towards Him. He asked if it was possible to have something of Ma's. She said, "Yes, on condition you promise to take very good care of it."

The devotee walked into the compound and then returned with the folded sheet we saw through the window. Immediately, I realised that this sheet was the relic Guruji requested from Ma.

We journeyed back to Rishikesh in silence and disbelief. He made it clear that He knew that we doubted His ability to receive a gift from such a great saint.

Hanuman appears before me

The next day was our final day at the International Yoga Festival, where Guruji was asked to present a musical performance. The stage was built in the middle of the Ganges. Guruji's performance was received with great enthusiasm. However, during his act, the organiser of the event needed everyone to take a group photograph, so she announced it a few times on the public address system. While all this was happening, a very interestingly dressed sadhu sat near me as I watched Guruji's performance. On his forehead, he wore a Sri Vaishnava tilak I had rarely seen in Rishikesh. The Tripura is the three lines drawn across the forehead by devotees of Shiva, yet this sadhu's attire did not match those of the Shaivites of Rishikesh.

There were also other curious things about him; his head and upper body moved unusually, the hair in the middle of his head was covered in sindoor, almost as if he had wiped his hand clean on his head. His hair was curly with more salt than pepper, his body muscular, and the clothing he wore was made from a really fine woven white linen.

He looked at me and said, "Your guru is from Mauritius." I said yes, and he kept looking at Guruji then looking at all of us pilgrims.

Meanwhile, the frustrated organiser, still trying in vain to gather everyone for the photograph, turned the volume off while Guruji was dancing. With the sound abruptly switched off, Guruji gestured questioningly. Someone had to explain to him.

As I stood up, I said to the sadhu, "We are going to take a photograph now." He looked at me and asked, "What is a photograph?" I said, "Come with me and you will find out." He reached out His hand to me, the way a child would. I took hold of it and walked with him lagging behind me to the place where the photograph was to be taken.

I continually looked back to see if he was okay as we negotiated the crowd of almost one thousand people. We had to climb onto a platform created to take the picture. I could feel his hand still in mine as I took the first step. I turned to see if he needed any help and even though I could feel His hand in my hand, he was gone. Feeling the weirdness of the situation, I looked for him in the crowd, but he was not there.

As Guruji came off the stage, we were all well-positioned for the photograph. As He climbed the few stairs, I watched Him stop for a moment and converse with someone who was not visible to the rest of us. When He was done, He joined us for the photograph and then we all dispersed.

The next day, on the bus to Vrindavan, Guruji said, "You are all so fortunate. One of the immortals was with you yesterday." This of course sparked our interest. "Which one?" I enquired. He turned in my direction and said, "He was walking with you and sat next to you."

I was confused for a moment because I remember that at the time the sadhu was speaking to me, Guruji was in the middle of the Ganges singing. Also, His eyes were closed. So how would He know who was speaking to me?

Then Guruji asked us to guess who this immortal person was. He gave us a couple of hints, asking who it was who promised to remain on Earth to take care of us and is considered to be the greatest devotee ever. Then we knew it was Hanuman.

I was dumbfounded. This was the first time I physically encountered Hanuman and considered it a privilege to have had a moment with Him.

Vrindavan

We reached Vrindavan a few days before Shivaratri. Guruji seemed very agitated. We travelled to all the sacred temples of Vrindavan completely oblivious to the greater plan at work. One day in the future, Guruji would build an Ashram here, and I would spend much time helping Him accomplish His mission.

I remember; all my thoughts and senses seemed heightened in Vrindavan, but with that came a strong reaction to dust that caused pain and congestion in my sinuses.

We kept meeting the same two ladies as we travelled from temple to temple. Later I learned these two ladies were devotees of Babaji Satyanarayana Dasa from the Jiva Institute. One of these Matajis invited Guruji to the Jiva Institute and He happily accepted.

We were invited for 7:30 pm, yet we went from place to place in and around Vrindavan, and by the time we arrived back at the hotel, it was already well past 8pm. I kept thinking 'When will we go to the Jiva Institute?' Guruji delayed until around midnight. During this time,

He was speaking to several people who were seeking His advice. We arrived at the Jiva Institute around 12.30am and everything had to be reactivated. The sitarist had to return, the food had to be reheated and fresh samosas fried for Guruji. All of this happened with great zeal and excitement.

On the morning of Shivaratri, Guruji wanted to see the Yamuna River, so we all set out on foot. Arriving at the Yamuna, having just been at the Ganges, I was a little disappointed. It was a small stream and the water looked dull and polluted.

This was the day the initiation ceremony of Yamunashree, a Swiss devotee, was to occur. I watched as she looked at the water in horror. It was so dirty, but Guruji put His hands in the water and sprinkled water on all of us.

Guruji seemed increasingly agitated. He completed the initiation and proceeded to walk back. As we followed Him, I stubbed my toe, so I looked for a rickshaw. There were only pedal rickshaws available, I climbed on one with one other person and pedalled away. Guruji was ahead and when we passed Him, He gave me the most unbelievable glare. Mortified, I paid for the rickshaw and walked the rest of the way to the hotel.

Guruji went to His room. As it was Shivaratri, everybody stood on the patch of lawn in the middle of the hotel. People started singing spontaneously. As we sang, the aroma of vibhuti started to permeate the air. The entire hotel was filled with the fragrance of vibhuti emanating from Guruji's room.

A few minutes later, He exited His room holding a beautiful, elongated lingam of smoky quartz. His mood seemed to have changed completely and He appeared more approachable.

The remainder of the time was spent recalling special events of the tour and doing a little shopping in Vrindavan until we departed for Delhi.

Guruji spoke a little about His plan for me, but not with any clarity. I did not know that this was the year He was to give me the great gift of being able to serve Him as a Swami.

Arriving back in South Africa, the incredible experiences with Guruji carried me through the next months. Many friendships were formed during that six-week pilgrimage with Guruji. Some remain to this day.

BECOMING A SWAMI

Settling in

The invitation to visit Bhakti Marga in Germany arrived as we were heading into winter in South Africa. Preparing all the documents required to apply for my visa was an extremely interesting, yet frustrating process.

We could not use any scanned or email versions of the documents and they had to be sent by courier. This information came from the German Embassy at the eleventh hour, when I thought I would be heading for the airport. The courier service did not deliver the documents in time, which meant we needed additional documents. I will never forget the declaration of financial obligation the administrators at the Ashram had to sign assuming full responsibility for me while I was in Germany.

I arrived in Germany with another devotee, and we went through passport control without much difficulty. Chandrikandra was there to meet us.

This was my first visit to Germany. Arriving at the beginning of summer, it was a welcome change from the freezing cold of a South African winter. I looked forward to experiencing the legend of the autobahns with no speed limit. As we drove through Frankfurt, negotiating our way towards the small village of Stefanshof, where Guruji had established His first Ashram in Germany, I took in the sights – buildings, cars, people and smells – and automatically compared it to my arrival in India.

During the one-hour drive, I watched as the city disappeared into fields of yellow and green. The rapeseed was in full bloom, and as we approached Stefanshof, I marvelled as we drove between fields of wheat, potatoes, and corn.

Arriving at the Ashram, we were warmly received and given a choice of bedrooms to sleep in. We then met everyone, visited the temple, and ended the day with an audience with Guruji. His demeanour was warm, and I remember thinking, 'Finally I am with you again!'

The cherry tree in the front yard was in full bloom and everywhere were signs of life and rebirth. Morning prayers, evening prayers, lunches, dinners, breakfasts … the days blended into each other. I often saw Guruji in the women's house, busy with relics or speaking to one of the Matajis. He spent much of His time there. We were not allowed to enter the women's house. I remember thinking how fortunate they were. I randomly met Guruji outside or about to enter the women's house and we would have a short conversation before He continued on His way. There was no real sit-down and talk. There was no time or need for it.

He attended evening prayers and gave interviews and Darshans on Thursdays. Often, He would give me Darshan first, then start laughing uproariously, as if He had seen something hilarious.

The power of mantra

To continue working on the issue of pride He told me that every evening I would sit in the temple and recite the Ugram Vigram Mahavishnum mantra. Some of the guys from the men's house would join me.

I remember the joy I felt when one day, as I approached Him for Darshan, He looked at me and said, "That is better." With this utterance, He showed me the transformational power of the mantra. I learnt that if we diligently use the tools He gives us, we can change those qualities He sees as a barrier to God-realization.

In all the time I was at the Ashram, He came to the men's house twice. Once to have lunch with us, and the second time to share the Gayatri mudras. It was really lovely being with Him in that setting, and I wished it could always be like this.

One day, Guruji announced that He had made a list of those who were to become Swamis, and that those people would have to do some preliminary training in puja and chanting in London.

Racial profiling

Flights were arranged then several of us headed off to London at His expense. Before we left, He warned us that some of us would be stopped at the airport. We flew with Ryanair to London which was a first for me. I had never visited the UK before.

At this time, South Africans did not require a visa to enter the UK. We landed and the Europeans I was travelling with cleared Customs and Immigration with ease. Now it was my turn. The questions asked _ I answered. The customs officer needed to know if I could support myself during my stay in the UK and through the course of the conversation, I realized she thought I wanted to escape South Africa.

It had become clear that I was being racially profiled, so I decided to answer her questions in such a way that would irritate her. She asked how much money I had to support myself, and then wanted to see how much I had in my bank account. I told her I did not have a bank account or a bank card and answered no to all the questions I should have answered yes to. At this point, she asked me to get my bag and to follow her. She asked if I was travelling alone, and I pointed to one of the devotees who lived in the Ashram in Stefanshof who was a few people behind me in the queue.

We were both held in the custody of the State, questioned, and cross-questioned in different ways. My bag was searched, and they found a little bag of powder. I explained what vibhuti was. She was satisfied with my answer but gave it a sniff anyway. After speaking to our hosts, we were released with apologies from the customs officer.

Preliminary training begins

We arrived at the Narasimha Temple in Feltham, where the training was arranged. Guruji organized a traditional South Indian Sri Mastava to show us the 16 steps of worship and the mantras that accompany it. This included all the rituals for daily worship of the deity.

We proceeded with the traditional method of memorising mantras step by step with our teacher from Sri Villiputi. It was incredibly difficult and took long to learn.

The world of traditional Sri Vaishnavism was so different from our world with Guruji. This teacher shared in detail all the rules; the do's and don'ts, the should's and should nots.

We sat in a circle on the floor and followed the call-and-response technique of learning. He would not allow us to write anything. Since we had no script to read from, our attention had to be completely present.

He explained at great length the procedures for everything from opening a temple to the performance of japa, as it is laid down in the Agama, the rule book governing every spiritual tradition in Hinduism. It was an incredibly intense time and it felt almost as if my brain was being heated and stirred.

Gradually the mantras and learning designed to shape students to hold Sanatana Dharma was absorbed. I was amazed at the process and how knowledge was transmitted in ancient times in India. I felt so privileged to be exposed to the gurukul system. The effort Guruji was making towards our spiritual education did not escape me. Even though it was really stressful and our teacher very strict, I appreciated every moment.

Towards the end of this time of learning, our teacher wanted us to demonstrate that we understood what we had learned. He was dismally disappointed when we made mistakes, especially when people were watching. He admonished us, insisting that we practice more to become proficient. By now, it was clear that Guruji was coming to London and that we would have to make the same presentation to Him. Our teacher used this to his advantage and reminded us how much effort and sacrifice Guruji made for us to receive this training.

Eventually, Guruji arrived, and we were ready to give our best to Him. He watched as we chanted. He smiled and corrected the one mistake we made. It was such an incredible moment to see something that would usually take much longer bear fruit in so short a time. He encouraged us to practice more. There was a crescendo of love and kindness. I remain eternally grateful to have experienced these teachings.

Passing on the learning

On our return to Germany, it was evident the rigorous requirements of initiation had spread through the Ashram.

Guruji called on all of us who received the training to inform us that it was our responsibility to pass the information we learned to the residents of the Ashram.

Getting started with Guruji's instructions, it seemed unbelievable that what took us weeks to learn, the women learned in a relatively short time. They did, however, struggle to learn it using the method we were taught; recitation, listening, and correction was not working so well. In the end, we wrote the mantras down and they found it was much easier to learn.

Decision time

Once again, Guruji called on us who were to be initiated. Looking at each of us in turn, He said, "Now is the deciding time.".

He explained it like this. Before initiation could take place, we would have to enter a period of silence in which we would discover how committed we were. This initiation was considered extraordinary and would take all of our focus, for the rest of our lives. We would now live only for God; we would now live only to accomplish Guruji's mission. In that process, we would be refined in our personal qualities, polished until we shone with His light. It would be far from easy, and so we needed time to reflect on the road ahead.

We began a silent retreat that would last ten days. We performed our spiritual practice, read the Srimad Bhagavatam and focused our awareness on Him in different ways. We went into isolation in different parts of the men's house.

It was a very interesting time because maintaining silence is not something I find difficult. I realized I should have read the Srimad Bhagavatam a bit slower since I had read the entire book by the third day. Re-reading it seemed boring, so I resorted to remembering different scenarios, replaying moments of Guruji chanting, and practising Kriya. I noticed my senses became quite heightened, particularly my sense of smell.

I learned that silence has its own frequency band in which the metaphysical qualities of life are experienced. I started feeling it on the fourth day when my connection to Him became more intense and palpable. I dreamt He was five times His size, and one of the people who was to take initiation with us was rotating a huge arati lamp in front of Him. He looked at us with incredibly piercing eyes and seemed ferociously beautiful, such that any movement He made could create or destroy multitudes simultaneously. I imagined that this must be how it feels at the beginning or end of a cyclone, or something equally powerful and unpredictable.

Simple things became fascinating; watching the sun rise and set, listening to the sounds of people walking around the building, hearing the birds and the machines harvesting wheat or ploughing the field. Silence changes perception.

On several occasions during these ten days, the reality of the commitment came starkly into focus, and I found myself wondering if I was ready for it. This thought was followed by the understanding that I was more than my doubts. These were just thoughts, and since the real Self was beyond thought, I did not need to pay attention to those ideas that would keep me limited.

During this time, Guruji had travelled to France, and the day He returned, He entered our room wearing vivid yellow. His beauty and power almost induced me to speak, but He cautioned me against it. I felt the reality of the dream I had of Him; although He stood before us in human form, I felt His size and majesty.

I followed Him out of the room, and as He walked up the stairs, I grabbed His hand from behind. He turned and smiled. I returned to my room and basked in the feeling of joy from seeing Him.

Initiation

The next day we woke early. There was some commotion as many people had arrived in Stefanshof for Guruji's 30th birthday. We were briefed on the logistics of our initiation ceremony before we set out to the location where it would be held.

It was a really cold morning when we met behind the temple in an open patch of land. There were several vessels filled with all the ingredients for Abhishekam. The principle behind this Abhishekam ceremony was total surrender to those being initiated. Guruji arrived and did not explain much more than to commence the Abhishekam puja. Ingredient after ingredient was poured on us. Milk, yoghurt, ghee, honey, sugar and panchamarit. I understood the significance of Abhishekam, yet wrestled with the notion that He was surrendering to us. Yet He was doing just that by installing Himself within us. I felt humbled by this trust He had in us. So many emotions moved through me, including a sense of unworthiness. He had already provided so much, and now this.

Next, He gave us our clothes, dressed, and named us. He gave us our authority as Swamis, which signified we now belonged solely to Him, and that the clear purpose of our life was to surmount every spiritual challenge that would arise.

As part of the naming ceremony, we underwent Pancha Samskara, one of the central rituals of the Sri

Vaishnava tradition. It is through this rite that one becomes a Vaishnava Swami. We received two branded embossings; one of the Shankara (the Lord's conch) on the left upper arm, and the Chakra (the Lord's discus) on the right upper arm. These embossings indicate that our bodies are dedicated to God and Guru. This also demonstrates our commitment to Upaya, which is the obligation to obtain knowledge that will grant liberation.

I spent the remaining time I had in Germany thinking about this awesome commitment, and the complete trust my beloved Guru had invested in me. As His birthday celebrations continued, I reminisced about all the significant life events that led up to this. I felt that little boy in the countryside who yearned to feel the presence of God. I felt him leaping with joy, because here he was, standing in the presence of God, starting a new life as a Swami. My gratitude goes beyond words and is felt only as an overwhelming, all-consuming Love from which I never want to recover.

THE RECKONING

Defences

There are times in every devotee's life when the mind is challenged to such an extent that its defences rise with a force that can seem impenetrable.

We have lived for aeons of time with rigid belief systems that keep us reduced; we have no idea who we are, who God is, where we are now and how we arrived here. Because of ignorance of the real Self and its existence beyond the body and world, we endure life within invented human identities. In other words, we live in delusion because we create ideas and belief systems that tell us how to think and how to act, and over time we think these ideas are a natural part of who we are. We weave them into our education system, into our familial and social networks. They become entrenched and difficult to challenge.

To aggravate things further, we become attached to the body and identify so completely with it that it is difficult to see ourselves in any other way. So trapped are we in this theatrical human tragedy that to attain freedom from it, we need help from Divine sources.

But when an Avatar of God appears, someone whose way of Being cannot be comprehended by us, we can only relate to them within the limited lens of our mind. We can only see them as we see ourselves. It is simply not possible for us to be any other way. We are blinded by ignorance and rely on them to hold our hands and show us the way out of the forest of delusion.

They see us with great clarity and can look beyond the human body to see precisely how our souls are ensnared. They work with us on an individual level to unravel the complex knot of ideas that keep us in ignorance.

But to work with an Avatar in this way takes trust, and trust means that we have to acknowledge our inability to understand how complex our entrapment is. We have to recognise the limitations and allow them to lead. However, this necessity for surrender is the first roadblock in our relationship with the Avatar. It triggers a colossal defence reaction and for a time, it is difficult to overcome.

I faced massive trials with Guruji in Mauritius and India, and many other devotees had similar experiences. But none of us was prepared for the reckoning that was to come. We were to face an ordeal that would make us question who we really were, and what it is that we wanted. It would dare us to make the journey from the mind to the heart because if we did not do so, we would not be able to travel further along this path with Guruji.

A new beginning

I returned to South Africa, inspired by my initiation, and keen to serve Guruji's incredible mission of awakening new devotees to the path of Bhakti Marga.

Before leaving Germany, I had several conversations with Guruji about what I should do or say. His reply was quite simple, "Let them know you are the boss now." Having never really spent time in the Ashram in Johannesburg because I was always moving from place to place, it was a very new experience being in one place for an extended period.

I talked to my fellow housemates, one who later became Swamini Vishwa Mohini and the other, a former Brahmachari known as Devangi. Together we built a strategy for the way forward and, with a great deal of excitement and fervour, we began implementing our plans. I have fond memories of our very first Yagna, a forty-day affair that embraced many wonderful devotees and followers.

A bomb drops

One day, I received a totally unexpected phone call from Guruji. It was the first time He had ever called me. He said words to the effect of, "They have chosen to follow their minds, over me." I had no clue what He meant and was shocked when He described an incident which caused His Swamis and other devotees to question who He was. He was disappointed but unsurprised. After all, He had foretold this event in India a year ago. My mind reeled as I remembered His words, "By this time next year, half of you will have left me." It happened just as He said it would.

The churning of the milky ocean

To describe the situation in this book would be an offence because the truth of what occurred is not available to the spiritually immature.

What I can say, however, is that what happened was a present-day depiction of the ancient story of the churning of the milky ocean. Guruji created an event that would remove the poison of doubt from the hearts of His current devotees. He wanted to create a shift in how they saw Him; He needed them to view Him through the heart, instead of the mind. Our journey *to* the Guru, and our journey with the Guru are two distinct pilgrimages. The journey *to* Him is with the mind. The next part of the journey can only be made with the heart because it is through the heart that God-realization occurs. With minds so ingrained by artificial ideas, we cannot make that shift easily. It is the shockwaves of devastating events like this one, that galvanise change.

From the mind to the heart

This event in Bhakti Marga history is of great importance to us today because it took us beyond the surface of our relationship with Guruji. It shifted the perspective from the mind to the heart of those who remained with Him. It must also be said that, of those who left Him, many returned years later, having seen their error, having made the journey from the mind to the heart in their own time. We each have different destinies, and some must take very different paths.

Like the devas, we human beings have lost our spiritual wealth and the power to live in the abundance of Love. And like the devas, we seek Amrit, that elixir that will free us from the miseries of this world. Most people, in their delusion, think that Amrit is found in material acquisitions. But those of us who have found Guruji, know that He will help us find the real thing. What we don't always know or accept, however, is that Amrit comes with a price.

During this time, Guruji dismantled the entire organisation and released everyone He initiated as Brahmachari. He intended to rebuild on different foundations. I remember speaking to Him on the telephone and asking Him why He chose to do it this way. His words were, "I cannot build on sand. I have to know who is with me." It was becoming obvious that His current devotees could not see Him for who He was and had weak expectations of Him that came from their limited human conditioning. He let it be known that those who were with Him, were to lay their limitations at His feet and to focus only on Self and God-realization.

There was so much flux, so many changes. We were faced with all the poisonous ideas that had surfaced during this event. We found ourselves examining our attachments – what were we still clinging to? How were we still enthralled by the outside world? What were our real motivations for being with Guruji? What did we want from Him? What self-serving ideas were tainting our 'service' to Him?

We were also faced with excruciating judgments and doubts; Is He for real? What evidence is there to support the claim of His Divinity? Why is He sometimes so harsh with us? Aren't men of God supposed to be kind all the time? Am I weak for following a guru? Should anyone follow a guru? What brought me here?

The fear was intense and agonizing. We felt as if we were floating rudderless on open, stormy seas. But Guruji was patient. He waited as we made the slow transition from the mind to the heart.

This journey cannot come about through a Satsang. It comes only when we face this kind of crisis where we are forced to tell the truth to ourselves. The most important question we asked was what brought us here. It was the answer that created the shift.

Every one of us, including those who left Him, recognised Him in their hearts. Whenever people asked

Him if He was their Guru, He would answer, "What does your heart tell you? All the answers lie there."

It dawned on me that I could never see with my mind, who Guruji truly was. With my mind, I find only logical arguments against Him. When I looked at Him from my heart, through the absolute all-encompassing Love He generated, I saw only Divinity. I now see things I could not see before because my mind no longer has authority. I live in His world. He is expanding my vision and opening me up to higher experience. I see now that everything is possible.

This is the gift He gives us all once we make that most important journey, from the mind to the heart.

A VISION OF LORD KRISHNA

Naiveté

In 2013, I joined Guruji on a pilgrimage that included a stop in Varanasi – an event that created a profound transformation in mindset for me.

Plunging into the depths

We arrived in Varanasi on the 8th of February 2013. It was a drama of a journey which had us travelling overnight by car from Bihar. But now we were in the presence of Guruji! The plan for that afternoon was to take a slow boat ride to Ashwamedh Ghat, to watch the evening Ganga Arti from the river vantage. My heart was full, and I relished the idea of this trip on the Ganges.

I sat with Guruji and about fifteen other people on the boat. Suddenly, I felt like my entire life was for nothing. Strange, unsettling thoughts arrived in rapid succession – I do not know who I am, I do not know where I'm going, there is no point to my existence, no point to existence itself, I'm useless, I spend my life doing useless things, I've never been of any use to anyone. It was as if I had plunged into the depths of my mind and was hit by an avalanche of derisory notions.

I looked for the source of this outpouring but could not find it. I was under attack by self-doubt, and I could not see a way to navigate out of this feeling. There was only desperate uncertainty and a sense of standing on the precipice of Hell.

That ominous sense of apprehension must have radiated from me, because when I tapped on Guruji's shoulder, He turned and asked me what was wrong. When I explained what was happening, He responded, saying, "You feel like this because your aim is not 100% fixed". I stared at Him for a moment, then said, "I do not know how to fix any aim, You will have to do it, You will have to help me." He simply replied, "I will think about it.

Baby Krishna appears

This gesture from Guruji did nothing to remove the storm in my head. I placed all my efforts into focusing on the Ganga Arti, despite how I was feeling, and found it beautiful. We returned to our hotel for dinner, and early the next day left for Prayagraj. The feeling persisted, but it was slightly more removed as if the obstinate thoughts were located in another room. In the early evening, about eight of us gathered in Guruji's tent. It was a joyful atmosphere, and Guruji's mood was elevated, almost playful, as we took turns reading aloud about the life of Radharamancharan Das.

Guruji called me to sit next to Him on one of the single beds in His tent. Swami Aniruddha sat near us meditating, while two devotees were busy pressing Guruji's feet. As I sat by His side, He pointed to the bed in front of Him and said, 'Look". I looked at the bed but did not see anything. "Look carefully", He said again, still I could not see anything. Without saying anything further, He reached over to me and pressed the right side of my face, to the left side of His face. In this position, our eyes were in a single row. Raising His arm to point at the bed again, He said one more time, "Now look carefully". Suddenly, I saw it. Appearing to me in the form of light and dark, a form of Krishna, no older than two or three years old, came into sight. An overwhelming feeling of joy flooded my entire being. I was flabbergasted! I examined with wonder, every detail of Krishna – the shape of His body as He lay asleep on His left side. His tiny hands holding His flute. His body covered from head to toe in jewellery. The peepal leaf upon which He slept, shone with the iridescence of a thousand diamonds. It seemed astonishing to me that such beauty could be created only out of dark and light. I looked questioningly at Guruji. This was not how the baby Lord Krishna is usually positioned on His peepal leaf. Guruji smiled, saying, "This is not how you are accustomed to seeing Him. Usually, His right foot is in His mouth".

The real goal becomes apparent

I was flooded by feelings of different qualities of love. Krishna was visible to me for at least 30 minutes. Eventually, I turned my back on Him, and Guruji invited everyone else to look. No one else was able to see. My attention was fixed on Him who had caused me to see. Guruji looked at me smilingly and said, "Now you know what to focus on", and in my mind I replied, "Yes, now I know that it is You I have to focus on".

My body suddenly reacted spontaneously, banging my head on the floor in front of Guruji's feet. I did not know what was happening and certainly had no control over my body's movements. Guruji sprung to action trying to save me from possible injury, by putting His foot between my head and the floor. Eventually, my body came to a point of rest, and the remainder of the evening passed in a blur of seemingly distant activity.

Processing

We headed out in the early morning to visit some of the sights. The noise from throngs of people was a stark contrast to the intimacy of the night before. I realised then that I needed to be alone to process all that happened. That afternoon before lunch, I found a quiet spot and settled down to meditate.

Immediately I closed my eyes, my mind became awash with all the desires I was harbouring at that time.

I wanted this. I wanted that. I had to do this, I had to do that. I needed to make this happen, I needed to make that happen. I had to be here, there, and everywhere.

As I watched the thoughts rush in every direction, I noticed they belonged to a world that did not embrace Guruji. What was worse, I was chasing these desires and did not want Him to know about them. It dawned on me how I lied to myself when I claimed I was giving myself to Him. Instead, I had a vision of myself serving Him with one hand, and holding what was 'my personal life' in the other hand behind my back. I was deluded enough to imagine that He was not in full awareness of what I was doing. I was deluded enough to think I could straddle both worlds.

I saw clearly how those desires had me chasing in directions opposite to the one He was trying to lead me to. In chasing those desires, I was serving myself. I felt the pull of them, I experienced the sensation of how my mind, ignorant of the truth, thought that meaning could be found in my desires. I realized that in entertaining those desires, in worshipping those empty aspirations, my mind was turned from Him.

All at once I saw the truth and *became* the truth. There is only Him. To follow Him means to focus only on Him. Nothing else. All desires must revolve around Him – the desire to attain Him, to love without condition, to serve without condition, and to move into deeper states of surrender. I knew then that I had to let go of the 'I' and allow Him to consume me. My whole life, all those desires, fell away in the instant of realization.

With my desires gone, a sense of peace overcame me, and I fell into a deep slumber.

Shortly after, Guruji found me asleep. As I opened my eyes, He sat down in front of me. I felt a flicker of shame as I looked at Him, but it quickly dissolved as He reached out to hold my left forearm with His right hand. It was in His eyes. He knew what I had been through. He lifted me up saying, "Let's go to lunch". His immense love and service towards me, His devotee, filled me with gratitude I am unable to articulate. I walked with Him. His job was done.

AT THE FEET OF THE GURU

The doorway to God

When it's time, we're all called to the feet of the Guru, because He is the doorway to freedom, the gateway to God. To move through the gate, He has to grant us God-realization. Before any of this can happen, we must realize the Self first. And with this realization, we must move beyond our dogmatic perceptions of life.

However, not everyone who is called takes to the idea of a Guru. With some, it takes a while before this can happen. In my role as Swami, I have seen us approach Guruji from different paths, and with different levels of spiritual awareness. Some of us fall at His feet immediately and for different reasons. Others refuse, keeping Him at arm's length until a time comes when the realization of who He is hits them unexpectedly.

Unfortunately for many people who resist their Guru, He has to work to break down their unconscious mental defiance.

Devotee A

Devotee A found himself involved in a very complicated legal entanglement. After a phone call inviting me to lunch at his mother-in-law's house, I wondered what they could want.

While eating the midday meal, they began to tell me the details of the entire story and requested I ask Guruji for His help. I was incensed and immediately asked why on earth would they think Guruji was no more than a handy resource to solve their problems. They were not even committed to this path and had not taken initiation as devotees, yet here they were asking for His help. I was angry because I had seen this too often; people simply using Guruji as a means to end their material problems.

Despite my feelings, I messaged Guruji and relayed how I had admonished them. In answer to this, Guruji called me almost immediately, His voice on the other side of the line was full of kindness and care. He very gently admonished me, saying, "It does not matter that they are not devotees, I am more than able to assist them. Don't pressure or push them." To this, I replied to Guruji, 'At least they should give something up'.

As I spoke on the phone to Guruji, I looked at the man with the problem and asked, 'What are you willing to give up?' Without hesitation, he replied, 'I will give up meat and alcohol'.

What followed were several experiences that were due to the grace of Guruji.

Looking for some kind of reprieve from the stress of the legal situation, this man and his family invited me to perform a fire ceremony (yagna) at their home. As I facilitated this, the man began to have strange visions.

In one of them, he saw himself in Guruji's presence, being bathed with several different ingredients, milk, rose water, cow's urine, kumkum, etc.

In another vision, he found himself standing in front of Guruji at a cliff's edge. Guruji lovingly looks at him, saying, "Whatever happens, keep your eyes on me. Only give your attention to watching me". In a few steps, Guruji is over the cliff, but not falling. He levitates in mid-air, then gestures for him to come. With every step back Guruji takes, he takes a step forward, until he is also over the cliff's edge, walking in mid-air, his eyes fixed on Guruji. Slowly they transverse the chasm until reaching the other side.

The message was clear. Guruji was telling this man he had to focus on Him, not the problem. He and his family had to surrender to Guruji, they had to take refuge only in Him. This was Guruji's way of making them see it was time to commit, time to bring them into His fold.

This man asked if I would please share these intimate inner experiences with Guruji, to validate the meaning he found in his visions.

This I did, and Guruji immediately confirmed that his visionary experiences were genuine and that he should be mindful to write them down.

One day, while I was visiting, this man came home from work around lunchtime when our meal was disturbed by the ringing of the doorbell. Looking at the surveillance screens, we see the Sherriff of the Court standing outside.

Upon investigating, he is told an order has been lodged to remove everything of value from the premises. His wife and mother-in-law immediately panic. In the middle of much flapping around, I ask them a series of questions; 'How is this panic helping the situation?' 'Do you like the feeling of panic?' 'Is it what you want to experience?' 'How about this, what can you do to remedy the situation?'

They are not able to answer my questions, so I say to them, 'You can begin by calming down and offering your feelings and the situation to Guruji. Lay them all at His feet.' After a few deep breaths, they sit down and hand over the entire situation to Guruji.

There is an immediate change of situation at the gate with a sudden shift in attitude from the Sherrif. Instead of pushing to remove the household contents, he instead looks for ways to resolve the situation.

Both this man and his family members are in absolute shock and awe. Clearly, this was a sign of Guruji's grace extending into their lives. From that moment, the situation resolved itself completely. Today, they are dedicated devotees.

Devotee B

I met Ben in India when I booked into an Ashram for a ten-day Vipassana. He was from Southampton in England, and we got along really well for the duration of our stay, although we never exchanged contact details when we left India. I did, however, tell him about a vision I had. I told him that two people would come to Southampton and that he would take Atma Kriya Yoga and be initiated by my very own Guru. He shook his head vigorously, arguing that he had grown up in the transcendental meditation movement and that he already had a Guru.

After being back in South Africa for a few months, I left for the UK to join Guruji. Ben was constantly on my mind; I just knew that he needed to be with Guruji. As soon as I landed in England, I searched for him online but to no avail. I knew the name of the university he studied at and when one of the UK devotees mentioned she was a professor at the same university, I asked if she knew Ben. I gave up when she said she had no recollection of ever meeting anyone with that name.

As part of Guruji's trip to the UK, His devotees had arranged a celebration of the guru. In the spirit of the Kumba Mela in India, Guruji had invited gurus and their devotees from as many lineages as possible. As the guests started arriving, I was walking towards the bathroom to redo my smudged tilak. I heard a familiar voice. It was Ben. He came towards me, and I asked, "What are you doing here, and why are you here?" He answered, "We were invited. Where else would I be?"

As we walked together, he told me that everything I predicted would happen actually transpired. Swami Tulsidas and Anushyua came to Southampton to teach Atma Kriya and Ben received the shaktipat from Guruji. He was back because He wanted to affirm to everyone that Guruji was indeed his guru.

Alone with Guruji, I started telling Him about Ben and how we met in India. I described the incredible 'coincidence' of meeting Him again here in the UK. He looked at me and said, "There is no such thing as coincidence." He also said that He would call on Ben when the timing was right.

After dinner that evening, Guruji asked me to call Ben, closing the door after he entered. I do not know who was more excited, Ben or me! About ten minutes passed before Ben emerged from the room, looking wide-eyed and shocked. He said, "He is my Guru. I told Him about my parents' guru and about my upbringing in transcendental meditation. He said it was good preparation and affirmed that I was His and He was mine and then touched me on my head."

Devotee C

Devotee C was a hard nut to crack. I find it a miracle that today, she lives in total surrender at Guruji's feet. She was quite successful in life and had built a good business with her husband. She always followed a spiritual path and had facilitated many workshops that helped others to see the world from a higher perspective. However, her heart started asking for more. She had a deep sense that something was missing, something more was needed to connect her with the Divine.

It was at this time in her life that we met through a mutual acquaintance. When she explained her spiritual predicament, I pointed out that while she had a relationship with God, it was not a personal one. She tended to relate to God as 'the Universe', or 'Spirit'. God, to her, was indefinable and obscure. What's more, she said she liked it that way, despite me pointing out that she was clearly not connected in the way her heart demanded connection.

When I told her it was time to meet my Guru, she baulked at the idea. As far as she was concerned, she would bow to no man, and the concept of a Guru was preposterous and embarrassing.

During our conversation, it also became clear that she had met a young Guru a few years back while living in Dubai and said it was a 'chance' incident, where she was introduced to someone regarded as a young 'saint'. I explained that it might have been Guruji, as He was visiting the region during that time. She remembered Him manifesting a cardamom seed for her, and chocolates for the other person present. I could see she had not appreciated the significance of the meeting, even after admitting that it remained on her mind.

She was adamant that gurus, or anything resembling Hindu spirituality was not for her. I found her views rigid. However, she continued to criticize me for 'blindly following others' and 'not thinking for myself'. I remember thinking she was a tough one and wondered if Guruji was playing games with me.

Some months after our first meeting, her business suddenly started falling apart in a big way. She was so distressed; I saw an opportunity for her to take Darshan with Guruji. I thought she should at least meet Him. I set up the meeting so that she could ask Him questions about the direction her life was proceeding. She agreed, saying, 'Well I want to save my business, and you never know, this hocus pocus might just work'. By now, I had heard it all but kept my nerve.

As she stood before Guruji, He asked her to pose her questions. She asked, 'What do I do to save my life from falling apart?' He answered, 'You have to surrender totally. Only total surrender is required from you.' She practically stormed off, wondering why she was stupid enough to queue for so long to hear this nonsense.

To her, to surrender any part of herself indicated weakness. She controlled everything, including her spiritual life. She lived by very clear and honest principles and believed she could keep everyone safe by following specific spiritual rules defined by her values, and by her 'negotiated' relationship with her indistinct God. If she did certain things 'right', the 'Universe' would protect her and her family. And she had very rigid ideas about what was right and wrong, in every walk of life.

A year later, her 21-year-old son died in a car accident. With that, everything crashed completely. Her business collapsed, she lost her home and car, and her and her remaining family had to move in with her parents. She hit rock bottom and became suicidal.

Everything she believed in was now up for question. This heavy blow to her psyche knocked everything off-kilter. We had many conversations, and from those, I realized that she had never lost her connection to God. She figured her previous relationship had not been authentic but did not know why. She still did not understand how to be in a relationship with Him.

I initiated her into Atma Kriya, and she started doing those exercises. Slowly, she found herself drawn to Indian spirituality, despite her views about it. She was more open now, after arriving at a place where she realized she did not have the answers to anything at all. Every resisting idea her mind threw at her, she challenged, following her instincts, even when her mind argued. Her son's death opened her heart, and she felt its guidance very keenly. She listened to the teachings of many Vedantin gurus before she fell at Guruji's feet. Her mind was determined and strong – a fortress. It took a heavy blow to get her to see Him for what He truly is.

To this day, she is eternally grateful for what He did for her. It stuns both of us that He would go to such lengths to bring us home, to free us from the prison of our minds. He came all the way to Dubai to make a connection years before she would meet Him again.

Today, she serves Him in absolute gratitude. We both still look back in awe of the circumstances which led to her being a devotee.

SEVA TO THE GURU

Seva

When we first embark on our journey with Guruji, most of us have little idea of the true meaning and deep implications of seva. Certainly, when I first started out with Guruji, I knew I wanted to serve Him, but often, like many Swamis, Brahmacharis and devotees, my motives were tinged with what I wanted for myself. I wanted Guruji to notice me, to see that I loved Him. Many others who felt a need to serve Him were also looking for acknowledgement that they were doing a good job; they wanted 'points' for the amount of work they were undertaking, and they strived to gain the prestige of certain positions within the organisation. Within Bhakti Marga, there was always the element of competition, of trying to out-do one another; we were all trying to stand out and be noticed. Guruji had His way of dealing with us, of shaming us in subtle ways, of holding up a mirror so we could see our flaws. He still made it clear that He loved us unconditionally, and that He expected this from us because we came to Him with various imperfections. It was what Seva was for – to show us who we are and offer us a way to move into our more authentic nature. He has always said that we often start out doing Seva in a very human way, very much influenced by our past and our more negative qualities, and that eventually, our Seva becomes purer.

A more profound significance

Superficially, the word 'Seva' can be defined as selfless service without any expectation of reward. But as we evolve, we realize a more profound significance means to serve without the presence of our human identity. To serve 'selflessly' means exactly that; to serve without a sense of 'I am doing this'. We get out of the way and allow God to do it all. Our past must disappear, and our wants must be absent. We undertake seva using our physical body so that our minds are elevated to a place where there is no sense of what 'I' want, or what 'I' need. We merge with the will of God. In these moments we are offered a glimpse of our Divinity.

I remember visiting Thiruvannamalai on one of our pilgrimages with Guruji when we made a stop at an orphanage that Kumari, one of Guruji's first devotees from Switzerland, supported for more than fifteen years.

On this visit, I discovered that Kumari had been an orphan herself and came from a very painful and broken past. She was keen to create a safe space for other children who had no parents. She was a gentle soul, and in the two days we spent there, we observed her generosity extend not just to people, but to dogs, cows, cats – any beings she felt needed help.

Guruji spent much time with her, discussing her motivations for doing this work. He was pleased with her work but knew she had to shift her focus and the reasons for doing it. At that moment, she was driven by her past. It was Her pain driving it. By helping orphans, she was feeding her own needs. Essentially, she was trying to heal her pain.

Once she understood this, Guruji closed His eyes and flooded the entire orphanage with His Love. It was almost palpable. Simultaneously, Kumari's past 'disappeared'. She was no longer haunted by her own pain, and her Seva was purified by Guruji's Grace. No longer was her work tainted by the idea of 'I am doing this for others'. It became 'He is doing this, and I am the vehicle through which He works.' In working this way, she made the right decisions, because they were not based on what she wanted as a child. She simply allowed decisions to be made by Guruji, whether she liked them or not. She became an open vessel, practising true Seva.

Guruji's Seva

To better understand what Seva means, we only have to look to Guruji as an example. He is an Avatar of God, a manifestation of the Divine in human form. He is here to serve those of us who have lost ourselves, and He works tirelessly to free us from the shackles of our minds.

He asks for nothing in return, for there is nothing we can offer Him. When He is in service, His human personality is absent. Only God exists, and it is He who does all the work.

In His selfless service, Guruji elevates our consciousness in many different ways. First, He works to find each one of us. He puts out the call, and our hearts respond. The yearning of our hearts, sometimes many years before we even set eyes on Him, and the explosion of love we experience whenever we see Him, provides the topic for the first lesson we learn; the heart is the true voice, and the only one worth listening to.

He meets us where we are, knowing the journey we have taken, recognizing our strengths and limitations, and being aware of exactly what we need. He offers shelter and provides the means through which we confront our shadow selves. He offers us Himself as the route Home, and He never disappoints.

In the spirit of Seva, Guruji travels constantly, giving regular Darshans in which we experience a direct interaction with God. This interaction creates shifts within us that eventually helps us to move closer to freedom.

Through Satsang, whether in-person or online, He imparts wisdom we can use in our everyday lives. He offers commentary from ancient scriptures making them accessible to contemporary minds.

He takes us on pilgrimages, offering us opportunities to take the Darshan of the saints and Deities of India. He regales us with their stories of struggle, hope, resilience, and God-realization, filling us with inspiration to keep moving on our journey to freedom.

He sings for us, opening our hearts to devotion and our minds focused on God. He dances, prays, worships and pulls our sluggish minds out of the stupor it has become accustomed to. He works relentlessly to free us. He lives and breathes to free us.

Seva of the devotee

Our attachment to the external world, and identification with the body, are the reasons we are so tightly bound to the wheel of karma. And it is Seva that extricates us from both. With this in mind, Guruji offers us a platform on which to serve.

All over the world, He builds communities His devotees are expected to sustain. Through the work it takes to build Temples and Ashrams, maintain them, and serve the community, devotees are performing duties designed especially for them. Many of us believe we are doing a favour to Guruji, that in some way we are helping Him.

The opposite is true. He is helping us to transform, and He does this by creating scenarios in which we can see our karmic motivations clearly. When we try to take control of a project, think we know best, compete with each other to be noticed, or do things to look good or serve our sense of inadequacy, all of these things rise to the surface during Seva. We see it in our conflicts with others, in our emotional outbursts and in our resistance to execute certain duties asked of us.

The best way to serve Guruji is by losing all these karmic motivations and begin acting for the welfare of others, by losing our sense of identity and allowing Guruji to work through us. In that way, we will execute any task, however menial, however invisible, and with whoever is part of the project. We stop picking and choosing and 'knowing best'. We stop thinking there is a 'right way' to do things. We stop thinking we are indispensable to a project. We stop imagining that things will go better if people 'listen to me'.

Instead, we accept all that He brings to us because we know that what He puts before us, we can learn from. Seva is not about us helping Guruji, because He does not need our help. Seva is Guruji's Grace in action. He needs us to know this.

JUST LOVE

A continuous thought

After all these years with Guruji, He is a continuous thought in my mind. I can feel His presence at every moment of the day or night. These days I cannot imagine how life was before Him. His care and continuous concern have been like no other friendship, no other relationship – not mother, father, or friend. It is certain and steady.

The past is past

In all the time we have spent together, I have never given an account of myself to Him. I have never said anything about my past, or where I came from, and He never asked. One day while I was visiting His ashram in Germany, I decided to write Him a letter, describing who I am and what my life experience has been.

I left it on His bed. In the letter, I shared some of the difficulties in my life and some of the things I still struggle with. He read the letter at some point but did not say anything to me until some time later. When He did address the issue, only Guruji and I were present. He said, 'You never have to write anything to me. You never have to explain yourself. I already know. Neither your past nor your present matter.'

In my mind, I wondered how they could not matter. I spent so much time living through the filter of my past, using that same filter to categorize people and place them in order of importance in my life. His statement made a big impact. Him loving me has nothing to do with how my mind imagines love works.

On one occasion, I walked into His room and saw several items I had gifted Him over some time. This was the first time He allowed me into His bedroom, and I said out loud, 'Wow you kept them!' He replied, 'Do you want me to give them away?'

What I am driving at is the unconditionality I have experienced in my relationship with Guruji. Yet there is an unmistakable line that separates us which makes it very clear who He is, where He exists, and who I am in relation to that. This has been made clear, not by anything Guruji has said, or any display made, but by the way He has conducted our relationship.

The glory of Him

In Canto 11 of the Srimad Bhagavatam there is a description of Krishna in Madhura. It portrays Him as a brazen beautiful young man, regal in status, surrounded by His friends as He makes His way to the palace of Kamsa. He walks in the knowledge of His magnificence, unconcerned about how anything will play out, since it is He who is the author of those events. This is how it feels when walking with Guruji through the narrow roads of Vrindavan. He is purposeful in His steps, in His direction, in His care of us as pilgrims. And this is how it feels wherever I walk with Him, wherever He and I find ourselves in the world.

It feels like He is a stream in a barren land and that wherever He goes, change must follow. Something as simple as Him stepping His feet in a place can change everything.

I knew from the first moment I saw Him that there was no one like Him. I now know that I will spend my entire life absorbing His love and working to emulate His behaviour. I can say I know what real friendship is because that is what Guruji has been to me – a friend like none other.

www.ingramcontent.com/pod-product-compliance
Lightning Source LLC
Chambersburg PA
CBHW052050220426
43663CB00012B/2516